Mastering
IT SERVICE MANAGEMENT
AND INFRASTRUCTURE LIBRARY
Concepts, Techniques, and Applications

Nikhilesh Mishra,
Author

Website
https://www.nikhileshmishra.com

Copyright Information

Dedication

This book is lovingly dedicated to the cherished memory of my father, **Late Krishna Gopal Mishra**, and my mother**, Mrs. Vijay Kanti Mishra.** Their unwavering support, guidance, and love continue to inspire me.

Table of Contents

Author's Preface

Welcome to the captivating world of the knowledge we are about to explore! Within these pages, we invite you to embark on a journey that delves into the frontiers of information and understanding.

Charting the Path to Knowledge

Dive deep into the subjects we are about to explore as we unravel the intricate threads of innovation, creativity, and problem-solving. Whether you're a curious enthusiast, a seasoned professional, or an eager learner, this book serves as your gateway to gaining a deeper understanding.

Your Guiding Light

From the foundational principles of our chosen field to the advanced frontiers of its applications, we've meticulously crafted this book to be your trusted companion. Each chapter is an expedition, guided by expertise and filled with practical insights to empower you on your quest for knowledge.

What Awaits You

- **Illuminate the Origins:** Embark on a journey through the historical evolution of our chosen field, discovering key milestones that have paved the way for breakthroughs.

- **Demystify Complex Concepts:** Grasp the fundamental principles, navigate intricate concepts, and explore practical applications.

- **Mastery of the Craft:** Equip yourself with the skills and knowledge needed to excel in our chosen domain.

Your Journey Begins Here

As we embark on this enlightening journey together, remember that mastery is not just about knowledge but also the wisdom to apply it. Let each chapter be a stepping stone towards unlocking your potential, and let this book be your guide to becoming a true connoisseur of our chosen field.

So, turn the page, delve into the chapters, and immerse yourself in the world of knowledge. Let curiosity be your compass, and let the pursuit of understanding be your guide.

Begin your expedition now. Your quest for mastery awaits!

Sincerely,

Nikhilesh Mishra,

Author

CHAPTER 1

Introduction to IT Service Management (ITSM)

In an increasingly digitized world, the seamless delivery of IT services has become the lifeblood of organizations across industries. From ensuring the availability of critical applications to promptly addressing user concerns, IT Service Management (ITSM) plays a pivotal role in optimizing IT operations and, by extension, the overall business performance. This introduction sets the stage for our journey into the realm of ITSM, where we will explore its significance, evolution, key principles, and the profound impact it has on modern organizations striving for operational excellence. Join us as we embark on a comprehensive exploration of ITSM and its transformative capabilities.

A. Definition and Significance of IT Service Management (ITSM)

In the contemporary landscape of technology-driven business operations, IT Service Management (ITSM) stands as a foundational discipline essential for the effective and efficient provision of IT services to organizations. To fully appreciate its

Mastering IT Service Management and Infrastructure Library

significance, one must delve into its definition and core principles.

Definition of ITSM:

ITSM is a strategic approach to designing, delivering, managing, and improving the way IT is used so that it can meet the ever-evolving needs of the organization. At its core, ITSM is about aligning IT services with the goals and needs of the business, ensuring that IT functions as a strategic partner rather than a mere support function. This involves the establishment of best practices, processes, and frameworks to optimize service delivery, support, and customer satisfaction.

Key Significance of ITSM:

1. **Enhanced Service Quality**: ITSM focuses on delivering IT services with consistent quality. By defining processes, roles, and responsibilities, it ensures that IT services are reliable and meet or exceed customer expectations. This is crucial for maintaining business operations and customer satisfaction.

2. **Alignment with Business Objectives**: One of the primary objectives of ITSM is to align IT services with the strategic goals of the organization. It ensures that IT investments and activities contribute directly to business outcomes, such as increased revenue, reduced costs, and improved customer experiences.

3. **Efficiency and Cost Reduction**: ITSM emphasizes efficiency through standardized processes and automation. By streamlining IT operations, it helps reduce operational costs and frees up resources for innovation and growth.

4. **Improved Incident and Problem Resolution**: ITSM provides structured approaches to incident and problem management. It enables IT teams to identify and resolve issues more quickly, minimizing downtime and disruptions to the business.

5. **Effective Change Management**: ITSM includes change management processes that help organizations implement changes in a controlled and predictable manner. This reduces the risk of service disruptions caused by changes or upgrades.

6. **Continuous Improvement**: ITSM encourages a culture of continuous improvement through practices like Continual Service Improvement (CSI). Organizations regularly assess and enhance their IT services, processes, and performance to adapt to changing business needs and technology advancements.

7. **Compliance and Risk Management**: ITSM helps organizations adhere to industry regulations and standards. It provides a framework for managing risks associated with IT operations and ensures that the organization remains in compliance with legal and regulatory requirements.

8. **Customer-Centric Approach**: ITSM places a strong emphasis on customer satisfaction. It involves gathering feedback, measuring service performance, and making improvements based on customer needs and expectations.

9. **Strategic Decision Support**: By providing data and insights into IT service performance, ITSM enables informed decision-making. It helps organizations allocate resources, prioritize projects, and invest in technologies that align with their strategic objectives.

10. **Competitive Advantage**: Organizations that excel in ITSM gain a competitive advantage. They can innovate faster, respond to market changes more effectively, and provide superior customer experiences, all of which are critical in today's fast-paced business environment.

In conclusion, IT Service Management (ITSM) is not merely a set of processes and practices but a strategic framework that empowers organizations to harness the full potential of their IT resources. Its significance lies in its ability to drive efficiency, alignment with business objectives, and continuous improvement, ultimately leading to enhanced service quality and a competitive edge in the market.

B. History and Evolution of IT Service Management (ITSM)

The history of IT Service Management (ITSM) is a journey that reflects the evolution of information technology and its integration into modern business practices. Understanding this evolution is crucial for grasping the significance of ITSM in today's technology-driven world.

1. Early IT Management:

The roots of ITSM can be traced back to the early days of computing when computers were large, centralized systems operated by a select group of experts. At this stage, IT management was focused on ensuring the availability and reliability of these systems, with little emphasis on user experience or alignment with business goals.

2. Emergence of ITIL:

The true foundation of ITSM as a structured discipline began with the development of the Information Technology Infrastructure Library (ITIL) in the 1980s by the British government's Central Computer and Telecommunications Agency (CCTA). ITIL introduced a set of best practices and guidelines for managing IT services, emphasizing the importance of aligning IT with business needs.

3. ITIL Versions and Widespread Adoption:

Over the years, ITIL went through multiple versions, each refining and expanding the framework. Key milestones include the release of ITIL v2 in the early 2000s and ITIL v3 (also known as ITIL 2011) later in the decade. These versions provided comprehensive guidance on service strategy, design, transition, operation, and continual improvement. ITIL's best practices gained recognition and were adopted by organizations worldwide.

4. Integration with Frameworks and Standards:

As ITSM matured, it became closely integrated with other frameworks and standards. ISO/IEC 20000, for example, is an international standard for IT service management that aligns with ITIL principles. This integration made it easier for organizations to achieve certification and demonstrate their commitment to quality IT service delivery.

5. Expansion into Modern IT:

The evolution of ITSM continued as it adapted to the changing IT landscape. The rise of cloud computing, mobile technology, and agile development practices prompted ITSM to incorporate new methodologies and approaches. Concepts like DevOps and Agile Service Management emerged to bridge the gap between development and operations, emphasizing collaboration and rapid service delivery.

6. Digital Transformation and ITSM 4:

In response to the demands of digital transformation, ITSM evolved again with the introduction of ITIL 4 in 2019. ITIL 4 embraces a more holistic and flexible approach to ITSM, recognizing the importance of adapting to a fast-paced, digital world. It emphasizes the integration of ITSM with emerging technologies, such as artificial intelligence (AI) and automation.

7. Beyond ITIL:

While ITIL remains a significant and widely adopted framework, the ITSM landscape has diversified. Other ITSM frameworks and methodologies have gained prominence, including COBIT (Control Objectives for Information and Related Technologies), Lean IT, and SIAM (Service Integration and Management). These frameworks address specific needs and offer alternatives or complements to ITIL.

8. Ongoing Evolution:

The history of ITSM is marked by its ongoing evolution and adaptation to the ever-changing IT and business environments. ITSM continues to be a critical discipline for organizations seeking to provide reliable, high-quality IT services that align with their strategic goals. Its future will likely involve further integration with emerging technologies, increased automation, and a continued focus on customer-centric service delivery.

In summary, the history and evolution of IT Service Management (ITSM) reflect the dynamic nature of IT and its central role in modern business operations. From its early origins to its integration with contemporary practices and technologies, ITSM has continually evolved to meet the evolving needs of organizations in the digital age.

C. Key Concepts and Principles in IT Service Management (ITSM)

IT Service Management (ITSM) is built upon a set of fundamental concepts and principles that guide organizations in delivering high-quality IT services. These concepts are essential for understanding the philosophy and framework that underpin ITSM practices. Let's delve into the key concepts and principles in ITSM in depth:

1. Service: At the heart of ITSM lies the concept of a "service." A service is a means of delivering value to customers by facilitating desired outcomes without customers having to manage specific costs and risks. In ITSM, services can encompass a wide range of IT functions, from email and network connectivity to application hosting and support.

2. Customer-Centric Approach: ITSM places the customer at the center of all activities. Understanding and meeting customer needs and expectations is a fundamental principle. This requires effective communication, service design, and continuous improvement to ensure that IT services align with the organization's goals.

3. Service Lifecycle: ITSM typically follows a service lifecycle approach, as outlined in frameworks like ITIL. The service lifecycle consists of stages, including service strategy, service design, service transition, service operation, and continual service improvement (CSI). This structured approach ensures that services are planned, designed, delivered, and improved in a systematic manner.

4. Processes and Practices: ITSM relies on well-defined processes and practices to manage services effectively. These processes cover activities such as incident management, problem management, change management, and configuration management. Processes ensure consistency and accountability in service delivery.

5. Continual Service Improvement (CSI): CSI is a core principle in ITSM. It emphasizes the need for ongoing assessment and improvement of services and processes. Organizations should regularly review performance data, identify areas for enhancement, and implement changes to drive continual improvement.

6. Alignment with Business Objectives: ITSM is not an isolated function; it exists to support the broader goals of the organization. Ensuring that IT services align with the business's strategic objectives is a critical concept in ITSM. This alignment enhances the organization's ability to leverage technology for competitive advantage.

7. Service Design and Strategy: The service design and strategy phases of the service lifecycle focus on defining and planning services. This includes determining service levels, understanding service costs, and ensuring that services are designed to be efficient, effective, and adaptable to changing business needs.

8. Incident vs. Problem Management: In ITSM, incidents and problems are distinct concepts. Incidents are disruptions in service, such as system outages, while problems are the underlying causes of incidents. Effective incident and problem management is essential for minimizing service interruptions and identifying root causes.

9. Change Control: Managing changes to IT services is a crucial concept. Change management processes ensure that changes are assessed, planned, tested, and implemented in a controlled manner to avoid negative impacts on service quality and stability.

10. Key Performance Indicators (KPIs): ITSM relies on KPIs and metrics to measure the performance and effectiveness of services and processes. These measurements help in making informed decisions, identifying areas for improvement, and demonstrating the value of IT services to stakeholders.

11. Governance and Compliance: ITSM includes governance practices to ensure that services adhere to regulatory requirements and internal policies. Compliance with standards and regulations is vital for risk management and maintaining the organization's reputation.

12. Service Catalog: A service catalog is a fundamental concept in ITSM. It serves as a central repository of available services, their descriptions, and associated service levels. The service catalog helps customers understand available services and request them as needed.

13. Agile and DevOps Integration: In modern ITSM, there's a growing emphasis on integrating ITSM practices with Agile and DevOps methodologies to achieve faster and more flexible service delivery.

In summary, the key concepts and principles in IT Service Management (ITSM) provide the foundation for effective IT service delivery. These concepts emphasize customer satisfaction, service quality, continual improvement, alignment with business objectives, and the use of structured processes to ensure reliable and efficient IT services. Adhering to these principles enables organizations to navigate the complexities of modern technology and deliver value to both internal and external customers.

D. The Role of IT Service Management (ITSM) in Modern Organizations

In the digital age, IT Service Management (ITSM) has evolved into a critical discipline that plays a central role in the success of modern organizations. Its significance extends far beyond the IT department, permeating the entire business ecosystem. Let's explore the multifaceted role of ITSM in today's organizations in depth:

1. Enabler of Business Strategy:

- **Alignment with Business Objectives**: ITSM ensures that IT services are closely aligned with the strategic goals and objectives of the organization. This alignment enables businesses to leverage technology effectively to gain a competitive edge, improve customer experiences, and drive growth.

- **Support for Innovation**: ITSM facilitates innovation by providing a structured framework for evaluating, implementing, and managing new technologies and solutions. It ensures that innovations align with business needs and are deployed efficiently.

2. Quality Service Delivery:

- **Reliable IT Services**: ITSM emphasizes the consistent and reliable delivery of IT services. It includes processes like incident management and problem resolution to minimize disruptions and downtime, ensuring that essential business functions remain operational.

- **Service Level Agreements (SLAs)**: Through SLAs and service catalogs, ITSM defines service expectations, including response times and availability, providing transparency and accountability to both IT and business stakeholders.

3. Enhanced Customer Satisfaction:

- **Customer-Centric Approach**: ITSM places the customer at the forefront. It ensures that IT services are designed, delivered, and continuously improved based on customer needs and expectations, leading to higher satisfaction levels.

- **Service Desk Excellence**: ITSM includes robust service desk practices, enabling efficient handling of user inquiries, incidents, and service requests. This contributes to a positive user experience.

4. Risk Management and Compliance:

- **Risk Mitigation**: ITSM incorporates risk management practices to identify and mitigate potential IT-related risks. By ensuring the security and stability of IT services, it safeguards the organization against data breaches, compliance violations, and financial losses.

- **Regulatory Compliance**: ITSM helps organizations meet regulatory and compliance requirements by establishing processes for data protection, audit trails, and incident reporting.

5. Efficient Resource Utilization:

- **Cost Optimization**: ITSM focuses on optimizing IT costs by implementing efficient processes, automation, and resource allocation. This ensures that IT investments are aligned with business priorities.

- **Resource Allocation**: ITSM enables organizations to allocate IT resources effectively, whether it's human resources, hardware, or software licenses, to maximize their utilization and ROI.

6. Change Management and Adaptability:

- **Controlled Change**: ITSM includes robust change management processes to control and track changes to IT services. This minimizes the risks associated with service disruptions and ensures business continuity.

- **Adaptation to Change**: ITSM frameworks like ITIL 4 emphasize adaptability and flexibility in response to rapid technological advancements and changing business requirements.

7. Continual Improvement:

- **Continuous Service Improvement (CSI)**: ITSM embraces the concept of CSI, encouraging organizations to regularly assess and improve their IT services and processes. This iterative approach drives ongoing enhancements in service quality and efficiency.

8. Data-Driven Decision-Making:

- **Key Performance Indicators (KPIs)**: ITSM relies on KPIs and metrics to measure service performance and the effectiveness of IT processes. Data-driven insights enable informed decision-making, allowing organizations to optimize their IT strategies and investments.

9. Integration with Modern Practices:

- **Agile and DevOps Integration**: ITSM has evolved to integrate with Agile and DevOps methodologies, enabling organizations to achieve faster, more collaborative, and automated service delivery in response to evolving market demands.

In summary, the role of IT Service Management (ITSM) in modern organizations extends far beyond traditional IT functions. It acts as a strategic enabler, ensuring that IT services are closely aligned with business objectives, fostering innovation, enhancing customer satisfaction, mitigating risks, optimizing resource utilization, and facilitating adaptability to change. ITSM is not just a set of practices; it's a vital driver of business success in the digital age, helping organizations thrive in an increasingly technology-driven world.

E. Benefits and Challenges of IT Service Management (ITSM)

IT Service Management (ITSM) is a powerful framework for delivering and managing IT services, but like any approach, it comes with its own set of benefits and challenges. Understanding both can help organizations make informed decisions about implementing and optimizing ITSM practices. Let's explore the benefits and challenges of ITSM in depth:

Benefits of ITSM:

1. **Improved Service Quality**:

    - **Consistency**: ITSM establishes standardized processes and procedures, ensuring that IT services are consistently delivered at a high level of quality. This consistency reduces service disruptions and improves reliability.

    - **Alignment with Best Practices**: ITSM frameworks, such as ITIL, are based on industry best practices.

Following these guidelines helps organizations avoid common pitfalls and leverage proven approaches for service management.

2. **Enhanced Customer Satisfaction**:

- **Customer-Centric Approach**: ITSM prioritizes the needs and expectations of customers. By aligning IT services with customer requirements, organizations can deliver more valuable and satisfying experiences.

- **Effective Service Desk**: A well-implemented ITSM approach includes a responsive service desk that can quickly address user issues and requests, leading to higher customer satisfaction.

3. **Efficient Resource Utilization**:

- **Cost Optimization**: ITSM emphasizes efficient resource allocation and management. This can lead to cost savings by reducing waste and ensuring that resources are used effectively to support business objectives.

- **Increased Productivity**: Streamlined processes and automation within ITSM lead to increased productivity among IT staff, allowing them to focus on higher-value activities.

4. **Risk Mitigation and Compliance**:

- **Risk Management**: ITSM includes risk management practices that help identify and mitigate potential threats to IT services and the organization as a whole.

- **Regulatory Compliance**: ITSM ensures that IT services adhere to regulatory requirements, reducing the risk of non-compliance and associated penalties.

5. **Strategic Alignment**:

- **Business Alignment**: ITSM aligns IT services with the strategic goals of the organization. This alignment ensures that IT investments and initiatives directly contribute to business success.

- **Innovation Enablement**: ITSM supports innovation by providing a structured framework for evaluating and implementing new technologies and services that align with business objectives.

6. **Data-Driven Decision-Making**:

- **Key Performance Indicators (KPIs)**: ITSM relies on KPIs and metrics to measure the performance of IT services and processes. Data-driven insights enable organizations to make informed decisions and improvements.

Challenges of ITSM:

1. **Complexity and Implementation Costs**:

   - **Initial Complexity**: Implementing ITSM can be complex, requiring a significant investment in time, resources, and training to establish processes and procedures.

   - **Costs**: The upfront costs associated with ITSM implementation, including training, software, and consulting services, can be substantial.

2. **Resistance to Change**:

   - **Cultural Change**: Shifting to an ITSM mindset often requires a cultural change within the organization. Resistance to change from employees and management can hinder adoption.

3. **Customization and Flexibility**:

   - **Overcustomization**: While ITSM frameworks offer flexibility, overcustomization can lead to complexity and difficulties in maintaining and upgrading systems.

   - **Balancing Flexibility**: Striking the right balance between standardized processes and flexibility to meet unique business needs can be challenging.

4. **Data Security and Privacy**:

- **Data Handling**: ITSM processes involve handling sensitive data, which requires robust security measures to protect against breaches and data leaks.

5. **Tool Selection and Integration**:

- **Tool Complexity**: Selecting and integrating ITSM tools can be challenging, as organizations must ensure that the chosen tools align with their processes and offer the required functionality.

- **Integration Challenges**: Integrating ITSM tools with existing systems and platforms can be complex and may require additional development efforts.

6. **Measurement and Metrics**:

- **Defining Relevant Metrics**: Determining which KPIs and metrics are most relevant to an organization's goals can be challenging, and organizations may initially struggle to collect and analyze data effectively.

In summary, IT Service Management (ITSM) offers numerous benefits, including improved service quality, enhanced customer satisfaction, efficient resource utilization, risk mitigation, strategic alignment, and data-driven decision-making. However, organizations should be aware of the challenges associated with complexity, resistance to change, customization, data security, tool selection, and measurement. Successfully addressing these challenges is crucial for realizing the full potential of ITSM and its positive impact on organizational performance.

CHAPTER 2

Understanding ITIL

In the rapidly evolving landscape of Information Technology (IT), the ability to manage and deliver IT services efficiently and effectively has become paramount for organizations seeking to thrive in the digital age. Enter ITIL, the Information Technology Infrastructure Library—a comprehensive framework that has emerged as the guiding light for IT Service Management (ITSM) practices worldwide.

In this exploration of ITIL, we embark on a journey to unravel the intricacies of this renowned framework, delving into its history, core components, and the principles that underpin its success. With ITIL as our compass, we navigate the complexities of ITSM, understanding its significance in modern organizations and its role in delivering services that not only meet but exceed the expectations of both business stakeholders and end-users alike. Join us as we demystify ITIL and equip you with the knowledge and insights to harness its power in your IT service management endeavors.

A. Introduction to ITIL (Information Technology Infrastructure Library)

ITIL, short for the Information Technology Infrastructure Library, is a globally recognized and widely adopted framework for IT Service Management (ITSM). Developed by the United Kingdom's Central Computer and Telecommunications Agency (CCTA) in the late 1980s, ITIL has since evolved into a comprehensive set of best practices, guiding principles, and processes that organizations use to design, deliver, manage, and continually improve IT services. In this in-depth introduction to ITIL, we will explore its origins, key components, and significance in modern IT.

Origins and History:

The roots of ITIL can be traced back to a desire for more effective IT management within the British government. Recognizing the need for standardized IT practices, the CCTA set out to develop a framework that could help organizations optimize their IT operations. The result was ITIL, which was first published in a series of books that provided guidance on various aspects of IT service management.

Over the years, ITIL has undergone several revisions and updates to keep pace with changing technology landscapes and the evolving needs of organizations. The most notable versions of ITIL include ITIL v2, ITIL v3 (also known as ITIL 2007), and

ITIL 4. Each version has built upon its predecessor, refining and expanding the framework to address contemporary IT challenges.

Key Components of ITIL:

ITIL is structured around a set of core components that provide a comprehensive approach to ITSM:

1. **Service Lifecycle**: ITIL adopts a service lifecycle approach, consisting of five stages:

   - **Service Strategy**: Aligning IT services with business objectives and defining the value proposition.

   - **Service Design**: Designing efficient and effective IT services, including processes, technology, and people.

   - **Service Transition**: Managing changes and transitioning new or modified services into operation.

   - **Service Operation**: Ensuring day-to-day service delivery, including incident management, problem management, and access management.

   - **Continual Service Improvement (CSI)**: Identifying opportunities for improvement and implementing changes to enhance service quality continually.

2. **Processes and Functions**: ITIL defines a set of processes and functions that organizations can adopt to manage various

aspects of IT services. These include incident management, change management, problem management, service desk functions, and more.

3. **Guiding Principles**: ITIL is guided by a set of principles that emphasize the importance of value creation, collaboration, and continual improvement. These principles help organizations make informed decisions and ensure that IT services align with business goals.

Significance in Modern IT:

The significance of ITIL in modern IT cannot be overstated:

1. **Improved Service Quality**: ITIL promotes standardized processes, leading to consistent service delivery, reduced disruptions, and higher service quality.

2. **Alignment with Business Goals**: ITIL ensures that IT services are closely aligned with the strategic objectives of the organization, enabling IT to contribute directly to business success.

3. **Efficiency and Cost Savings**: By optimizing processes and resource utilization, ITIL helps organizations operate more efficiently, reducing costs and freeing up resources for innovation.

4. **Risk Management**: ITIL's risk management practices help

organizations identify and mitigate potential IT-related risks, safeguarding against disruptions and security breaches.

5. **Customer Satisfaction**: ITIL's customer-centric approach leads to higher customer satisfaction by meeting user needs and expectations.

6. **Adaptability**: ITIL has evolved to integrate with modern practices like Agile and DevOps, ensuring that ITSM remains relevant in a fast-paced, dynamic IT environment.

In conclusion, ITIL is a foundational framework for IT Service Management that has evolved over decades to provide organizations with a structured and holistic approach to delivering IT services. Its key components, guiding principles, and adaptability make it an invaluable resource for organizations seeking to enhance service quality, align IT with business goals, and stay competitive in the ever-changing world of IT.

B. History and Development of ITIL (Information Technology Infrastructure Library)

The history and development of ITIL trace the evolution of IT Service Management (ITSM) practices from rudimentary IT operations to a sophisticated, globally recognized framework for delivering high-quality IT services. Understanding this journey is essential to appreciate the significance of ITIL in modern IT. Let's delve into the comprehensive history of ITIL:

1980s: The Birth of ITIL:

- **Government Origins**: ITIL originated in the late 1980s within the United Kingdom's Central Computer and Telecommunications Agency (CCTA), a government agency tasked with providing IT services to government departments.

- **Need for Standardization**: The CCTA recognized the need for standardized IT practices to improve the efficiency, effectiveness, and accountability of IT service delivery across government organizations.

- **ITIL v1**: The CCTA released the first version of ITIL, known as ITIL v1, which comprised a series of books, each addressing a specific aspect of IT service management.

1990s: Global Adoption:

- **Emergence of IT Service Management**: ITIL gained recognition beyond government circles and started being adopted by private-sector organizations. ITSM as a discipline began to take shape.

- **ITIL v2**: Building on the success of ITIL v1, ITIL v2 was introduced in the early 2000s. It incorporated additional processes and guidelines, including a more comprehensive

Mastering IT Service Management and Infrastructure Library

service lifecycle approach.

2000s: Maturation and Expansion:

- **Widespread Adoption**: ITIL v2 became widely adopted globally, and organizations increasingly saw the value of aligning IT services with business objectives.

- **ITIL v3 (ITIL 2007)**: In 2007, ITIL v3 was released, introducing the service lifecycle concept. It emphasized the importance of end-to-end service management and included five core publications: Service Strategy, Service Design, Service Transition, Service Operation, and Continual Service Improvement (CSI).

2010s: Evolution and Integration:

- **ITIL Practitioner**: In 2016, ITIL Practitioner was introduced as a guide to bridging the gap between ITIL theory and practical implementation. It provided guidance on adopting and adapting ITIL practices to real-world scenarios.

- **ITIL 4**: ITIL 4, released in 2019, marked a significant shift in ITIL's approach. It modernized the framework to align with contemporary IT practices, such as Agile, DevOps, and digital transformation. ITIL 4 introduced a more holistic service value system (SVS) and emphasized the importance of co-creation of value with customers.

Key Milestones and Themes:

- **Standardization**: ITIL aimed to standardize IT practices, making them consistent and repeatable across organizations and industries.

- **Customer-Centric Approach**: Over time, ITIL evolved to place a stronger emphasis on understanding and meeting customer needs, ultimately leading to higher customer satisfaction.

- **Service Lifecycle**: The concept of the service lifecycle, introduced in ITIL v3, emphasizes the end-to-end management of IT services, from initial strategy to continual improvement.

- **Adaptation and Integration**: ITIL has continually adapted to accommodate emerging practices like Agile, DevOps, and Lean IT, ensuring its relevance in a rapidly changing IT landscape.

Global Influence:

- **Global Adoption**: ITIL has become the de facto standard for ITSM, adopted by organizations worldwide. It has also influenced other ITSM frameworks and standards.

- **Certification and Training**: ITIL certification programs and training have become popular, helping IT professionals gain

Mastering IT Service Management and Infrastructure Library

expertise in ITSM practices.

In conclusion, the history and development of ITIL reflect its evolution from a government initiative to a global framework for IT Service Management. ITIL's journey has been characterized by a commitment to standardization, a customer-centric approach, the introduction of the service lifecycle concept, and adaptability to contemporary IT practices. As IT continues to evolve, ITIL remains a foundational and adaptable framework for organizations seeking to deliver value-driven IT services.

C. ITIL Framework Components: Building Blocks of Effective IT Service Management

The ITIL (Information Technology Infrastructure Library) framework is a comprehensive set of best practices and guidelines for IT Service Management (ITSM). It comprises several core components that collectively provide organizations with a structured approach to designing, delivering, managing, and continually improving IT services. Let's delve into the key components of the ITIL framework:

1. Service Lifecycle:

- **Service Strategy**: This phase focuses on defining the IT service strategy, aligning IT with business objectives, and understanding customer needs and market trends. Key components include service portfolio management, demand management, and financial management for IT services.

- **Service Design**: In this phase, IT services are designed based on the strategy defined in the previous phase. It includes designing processes, technology, and metrics to meet business needs. Key components include service catalog management, service level management, and capacity management.

- **Service Transition**: Service transition involves managing changes, ensuring smooth service transitions, and controlling risks associated with changes. It includes processes like change management, release and deployment management, and knowledge management.

- **Service Operation**: This phase is focused on delivering and managing services on a day-to-day basis. It includes processes like incident management, problem management, request fulfillment, and access management.

- **Continual Service Improvement (CSI)**: CSI is a cross-lifecycle phase that focuses on measuring, analyzing, and improving IT services and processes. It promotes a culture of continual improvement and aligns with Deming's Plan-Do-Check-Act (PDCA) cycle.

2. Processes:

ITIL defines a set of processes that are crucial for effective ITSM. These processes are organized into different categories:

- **Service Strategy Processes**: Include service portfolio management, financial management for IT services, demand management, and business relationship management.

- **Service Design Processes**: Encompass service catalog management, service level management, capacity management, availability management, IT service continuity management, and information security management.

- **Service Transition Processes**: Involve change management, service asset and configuration management, release and deployment management, knowledge management, and transition planning and support.

- **Service Operation Processes**: Include incident management, problem management, request fulfillment, event management, and access management.

- **Continual Service Improvement (CSI) Processes**: Focus on CSI register, service measurement and reporting, service review, and process evaluation.

3. Functions:

ITIL recognizes several IT functions that play vital roles within the IT organization:

- **Service Desk**: The single point of contact for users, responsible for handling incidents, service requests, and providing information.

- **Technical Management**: Responsible for technical expertise and overall IT infrastructure.

- **Application Management**: Manages applications throughout their lifecycle, from development to retirement.

- **IT Operations Management**: Handles day-to-day operational activities, such as server and network administration.

- **Request Fulfillment**: Focuses on fulfilling service requests from users.

4. Roles and Responsibilities:

ITIL defines various roles and responsibilities within ITSM processes and functions. Examples include the Service Owner, who is responsible for the end-to-end delivery of a specific IT service, and the Change Advisory Board (CAB), which assesses and approves changes.

5. Guiding Principles:

ITIL is guided by a set of principles that underpin its practices. These principles include focusing on value, designing for experience, starting where you are, working holistically, progressing iteratively, and keeping it simple and practical.

6. Service Value System (SVS):

In ITIL 4, the concept of the Service Value System (SVS) was introduced. It provides a holistic view of how all components work together to create value for the organization and its customers. The SVS includes the Service Value Chain, which outlines the key activities involved in creating value, and other components like the guiding principles and governance.

7. Practices:

ITIL 4 introduced the concept of practices, which are sets of organizational resources designed for performing work or achieving an objective. Examples include incident management, problem management, change control, and service level management.

In conclusion, the ITIL framework consists of multiple interconnected components, including the service lifecycle, processes, functions, roles, guiding principles, the Service Value System (SVS), and practices. Together, these components provide organizations with a comprehensive and adaptable approach to ITSM, enabling them to deliver high-quality IT services that align with business goals and customer needs.

D. ITIL Service Lifecycle Phases: A Comprehensive Guide

The ITIL (Information Technology Infrastructure Library) framework is structured around a set of five core service lifecycle phases. These phases provide a systematic and structured approach to managing IT services throughout their entire lifecycle. Each phase addresses specific aspects of service management and contributes to the overall delivery of high-quality IT services. Let's explore each of the ITIL service lifecycle phases in depth:

1. Service Strategy:

Objective: The Service Strategy phase sets the foundation for effective IT service management by aligning IT services with the organization's business objectives and customer needs.

Key Activities:

- **Service Portfolio Management**: This involves defining and managing the portfolio of services offered by the organization. It includes categorizing services, analyzing their value, and deciding whether to invest, maintain, or retire them.

- **Demand Management**: Demand management ensures that IT services are provided in the right quantity and quality to meet customer needs. It involves understanding customer demand patterns and influencing demand to optimize resource utilization.

- **Financial Management for IT Services**: This process involves budgeting, accounting, and charging for IT services. It ensures that the costs and value of services are understood and controlled.

- **Business Relationship Management**: Establishing and maintaining strong relationships with customers and stakeholders is critical. This process focuses on understanding customer needs, managing expectations, and delivering value.

2. Service Design:

Objective: The Service Design phase focuses on designing IT services that meet business requirements and are efficient, effective, and adaptable.

Key Activities:

- **Service Catalog Management**: Creating and maintaining a service catalog that lists all available services and their details, including service descriptions, service levels, and pricing.

- **Service Level Management**: Defining and managing service level agreements (SLAs) and operational level agreements (OLAs) to ensure that services meet agreed-upon levels of performance and availability.

- **Capacity Management**: Ensuring that IT resources (e.g., servers, storage, and network) are adequately sized to support the delivery of services.

- **Availability Management**: Ensuring that IT services are available when needed by minimizing downtime and disruptions.

- **IT Service Continuity Management**: Preparing for and recovering from disasters or service interruptions to maintain business operations.

3. Service Transition:

Objective: The Service Transition phase focuses on managing changes to IT services and transitioning new or modified services into operation.

Key Activities:

- **Change Management**: Controlling and managing changes to IT services to minimize the risk of disruptions and negative impacts.

- **Service Asset and Configuration Management (SACM)**: Identifying, tracking, and managing configuration items (CIs) to ensure accurate and up-to-date information on IT assets.

- **Release and Deployment Management**: Planning and managing the release and deployment of new or updated services and software.

- **Knowledge Management**: Capturing, storing, and sharing knowledge and information to improve decision-making and service quality.

4. Service Operation:

Objective: The Service Operation phase focuses on delivering and managing IT services on a day-to-day basis to ensure they meet customer needs and are reliable and efficient.

Key Activities:

- **Incident Management**: Restoring normal service operations as quickly as possible following incidents and minimizing the impact on business operations.

- **Problem Management**: Identifying and resolving the root causes of recurring incidents to prevent them from happening again.

- **Request Fulfillment**: Fulfilling service requests from users, such as access requests or service inquiries.

- **Event Management**: Monitoring and managing events and alerts to detect and respond to potential issues or exceptions.

- **Access Management**: Managing user access to IT services and ensuring that authorized users have the appropriate levels of access.

5. Continual Service Improvement (CSI):

Objective: The Continual Service Improvement phase emphasizes the need for ongoing assessment and improvement of IT services and processes.

Key Activities:

- **CSI Principles and Concepts**: Understanding the key principles and concepts of CSI, including the Deming Cycle (Plan-Do-Check-Act) for continual improvement.

- **The CSI Approach**: Following a structured approach to identify opportunities for improvement, define objectives, and measure progress.

- **Key Metrics and Measurements**: Defining and monitoring key performance indicators (KPIs) and metrics to assess the effectiveness of IT services and processes.

- **Implementing CSI in ITSM**: Implementing improvement

initiatives and projects to enhance service quality and efficiency.

- **Continuous Improvement Culture**: Promoting a culture of continual improvement within the organization to drive ongoing enhancements in service delivery.

In summary, the five ITIL service lifecycle phases provide a structured approach to managing IT services from initial strategy and design to transition, day-to-day operation, and continual improvement. By following these phases and associated processes, organizations can ensure that their IT services are aligned with business goals, efficient, and responsive to changing customer needs and market dynamics.

E. ITIL Service Value System (SVS): Unleashing the Power of Service Management

The ITIL (Information Technology Infrastructure Library) Service Value System (SVS) is a critical component introduced in ITIL 4, which represents a significant evolution from previous versions of the framework. The SVS provides a holistic and flexible approach to understanding how all the elements and activities within an organization work together to create value for its customers and stakeholders. In this in-depth exploration, we'll delve into the key aspects of the ITIL SVS.

Components of the ITIL Service Value System (SVS):

1. **Service Value Chain (SVC):**

   - **Plan**: This is where the organization strategizes and plans its service delivery. It involves defining the vision, creating a roadmap, and setting objectives to deliver value.

   - **Engage**: Engaging with customers and stakeholders is essential for understanding their needs and ensuring that services are designed to meet those needs effectively.

   - **Design and Transition**: This phase involves designing, building, and transitioning services. It encompasses activities related to service design, transition, and change management.

   - **Obtain and Build**: Acquiring the necessary resources (such as people, technology, and partners) to deliver services is crucial. Building and maintaining the infrastructure and capabilities needed for service delivery also fall into this phase.

   - **Deliver and Support**: The final phase focuses on the actual delivery and support of services. It includes service desk activities, incident resolution, and fulfillment of service requests.

- **Monitor and Improve**: Continuous monitoring of services and service delivery is vital for identifying areas of improvement. This phase includes activities related to performance measurement, monitoring, and continual improvement.

2. **Guiding Principles**:

- **Focus on Value**: All activities and decisions should aim to deliver value to the organization and its customers.

- **Start Where You Are**: Organizations should use their existing capabilities and assets as a starting point for improvement.

- **Progress Iteratively with Feedback**: Continuous improvement involves making incremental changes based on feedback and learning from experience.

- **Collaborate and Promote Visibility**: Collaboration among teams and transparency in communication are essential for successful service management.

- **Think and Work Holistically**: Consider the entire service value chain and system when making decisions and taking actions.

- **Keep it Simple and Practical**: Simplicity should be pursued in all activities to avoid unnecessary complexity.

- **Optimize and Automate**: Automation can improve efficiency and reduce the risk of errors.

3. **Service Value Stream (SVS):**

The Service Value Stream represents the specific sequence of steps that an organization uses to deliver a service to a customer or stakeholder. It outlines the activities, workflows, and interactions that occur during the service delivery process.

4. **Service Chain (Chain of Activities):**

The Service Chain represents a set of activities that work together to deliver a specific outcome. It includes various practices, processes, and roles involved in delivering a service.

Key Aspects of the ITIL SVS:

- **Value Co-Creation**: The ITIL SVS emphasizes that value is not solely created by the service provider; it is co-created with customers and other stakeholders. This highlights the importance of understanding customer needs and expectations.

- **Flexibility and Adaptability**: The SVS is designed to be flexible and adaptable to different contexts and industries. It provides organizations with a customizable framework to suit their unique requirements.

- **Integration with Other Components**: The SVS integrates with other ITIL components, such as the Service Value Chain, Guiding Principles, and Practices, to create a comprehensive approach to service management.

- **Continual Improvement**: The ITIL SVS promotes a culture of continual improvement, aligning with the overall ITIL philosophy. Organizations are encouraged to regularly assess and enhance their service management practices.

In conclusion, the ITIL Service Value System (SVS) is a central component of ITIL 4 that provides a holistic and flexible approach to service management. It focuses on value creation, collaboration, and continual improvement, ensuring that organizations can deliver high-quality services that meet customer needs and contribute to their success. By embracing the ITIL SVS, organizations can navigate the complexities of the modern IT landscape with a customer-centric and value-driven mindset.

F. Key ITIL Practices and Processes: Building Blocks of Effective Service Management

ITIL (Information Technology Infrastructure Library) is a

framework for IT Service Management (ITSM) that provides organizations with a set of best practices and processes to design, deliver, manage, and continually improve IT services. Key ITIL practices and processes are the foundation of this framework, offering a structured approach to ensuring the quality and efficiency of IT services. In this in-depth exploration, we'll delve into some of the most essential ITIL practices and processes:

1. Incident Management:

Objective: Incident Management focuses on restoring normal service operations as quickly as possible following incidents to minimize the impact on business operations.

Key Activities:

- **Incident Identification and Logging**: Recording details of incidents, including their impact and urgency.

- **Categorization and Prioritization**: Classifying incidents based on predefined categories and assigning priorities to them.

- **Incident Resolution**: Investigating, diagnosing, and resolving incidents to restore service.

- **Communication**: Keeping stakeholders informed about the progress of incident resolution.

- **Incident Closure**: Confirming that incidents are resolved to the satisfaction of the user and documenting the details.

2. Problem Management:

Objective: Problem Management focuses on identifying and resolving the root causes of recurring incidents to prevent them from happening again.

Key Activities:

- **Problem Identification**: Identifying and recording problems through analysis of incidents and trends.

- **Problem Classification and Categorization**: Classifying problems based on their nature and impact.

- **Root Cause Analysis**: Investigating problems to determine their underlying causes.

- **Problem Resolution**: Developing and implementing solutions or workarounds to resolve problems.

- **Change Management**: Coordinating with Change Management to ensure that solutions are effectively implemented.

3. Change Management:

Objective: Change Management is responsible for controlling and managing changes to IT services to minimize the risk of disruptions and negative impacts on business operations.

Key Activities:

- **Change Request Submission**: Receiving and documenting change requests from various sources.

- **Change Assessment and Prioritization**: Assessing proposed changes to determine their impact and priority.

- **Change Approval and Authorization**: Reviewing and approving changes based on predefined criteria.

- **Change Implementation**: Coordinating and executing the changes, ensuring that they are tested and validated.

- **Change Review and Closure**: Evaluating the success of the changes and closing the change records.

4. Service Level Management (SLM):

Objective: Service Level Management focuses on defining, documenting, and managing service level agreements (SLAs) and operational level agreements (OLAs) to ensure that services meet agreed-upon levels of performance and availability.

Key Activities:

- **Service Level Agreement (SLA) Definition**: Defining SLAs that specify service expectations, including response times, availability, and performance.

- **Service Level Monitoring and Reporting**: Monitoring services against SLAs and generating reports to assess compliance.

- **Service Improvement**: Identifying opportunities for service improvement and implementing changes as needed.

5. Service Catalog Management:

Objective: Service Catalog Management involves creating and maintaining a service catalog that lists all available services and their details, including service descriptions, service levels, and pricing.

Key Activities:

- **Service Catalog Creation**: Creating a catalog of IT services offered by the organization.

- **Service Catalog Maintenance**: Ensuring that the service catalog is kept up to date with accurate information.

- **Service Request Fulfillment**: Handling service requests from users based on the information in the catalog.

6. Knowledge Management:

Objective: Knowledge Management involves capturing, storing, and sharing knowledge and information to improve decision-making and service quality.

Key Activities:

- **Knowledge Capture**: Collecting and documenting knowledge from various sources, such as incidents and problems.

- **Knowledge Storage and Retrieval**: Storing knowledge in a structured manner and making it easily accessible to relevant personnel.

- **Knowledge Sharing**: Promoting the sharing of knowledge and best practices among teams.

7. Continual Improvement:

Objective: Continual Improvement is a cross-lifecycle process that focuses on measuring, analyzing, and improving IT services and processes.

Key Activities:

- **CSI Register**: Maintaining a register of improvement opportunities and initiatives.

- **Service Measurement and Reporting**: Defining and collecting key performance indicators (KPIs) and metrics to assess service performance.

- **Service Review**: Regularly reviewing services to identify areas for improvement.

- **Process Evaluation**: Evaluating ITSM processes to identify inefficiencies and areas for enhancement.

These key ITIL practices and processes provide organizations with a structured approach to managing IT services, addressing incidents, preventing problems, controlling changes, defining service levels, maintaining service catalogs, managing knowledge, and continually improving service quality. When effectively implemented, they contribute to efficient IT service delivery and alignment with business goals.

CHAPTER 3

ITIL Service Strategy

In the realm of IT Service Management (ITSM), a well-defined strategy is the compass that guides organizations toward their desired goals and outcomes. ITIL Service Strategy, a pivotal phase within the ITIL framework, serves as this guiding compass, illuminating the path to effective and value-driven IT service delivery. In this introductory exploration of ITIL Service Strategy, we embark on a journey to understand its significance, principles, and methodologies. Join us as we unveil the blueprint for ITSM success and delve into the strategic core of ITIL.

A. Service Strategy Principles in ITIL: The Foundation for Effective IT Service Management

Service Strategy is one of the core phases within the ITIL (Information Technology Infrastructure Library) framework. It plays a pivotal role in shaping an organization's approach to IT Service Management (ITSM) and aligning IT services with its business objectives. At the heart of ITIL Service Strategy lie several fundamental principles that serve as the guiding light for effective IT service delivery. In this in-depth exploration, we'll

Mastering IT Service Management and Infrastructure Library delve into these critical Service Strategy principles:

1. Value Creation through Services:

- **Principle**: The primary objective of IT services is to create value for both the organization and its customers. This value can take various forms, including increased efficiency, improved customer satisfaction, cost savings, and revenue generation.

- **Significance**: By focusing on value creation, organizations can ensure that their IT services are not just technical solutions but valuable assets that contribute to the achievement of business goals.

2. Defining Clear Service Assets and Service Constraints:

- **Principle**: Effective Service Strategy involves identifying and defining the organization's service assets (resources, capabilities, and knowledge) and service constraints (limitations and restrictions).

- **Significance**: Understanding service assets helps organizations leverage their strengths, while acknowledging constraints allows them to plan for and mitigate potential limitations in service delivery.

3. Balancing Supply and Demand:

- **Principle**: Service Strategy seeks to strike a balance between the supply of IT services and the demand from customers and stakeholders. It aims to ensure that services are delivered efficiently and effectively, meeting customer needs without overcommitting resources.

- **Significance**: Achieving this balance is crucial for optimizing resource utilization, cost management, and customer satisfaction.

4. Service Portfolio Management:

- **Principle**: Service Strategy includes managing the organization's service portfolio, which comprises all services, including those in development, live operation, and retirement.

- **Significance**: Service Portfolio Management allows organizations to make informed decisions about which services to invest in, maintain, or retire based on their strategic objectives and customer demand.

5. Service Provider Types and Strategies:

- **Principle**: ITIL recognizes different types of service providers, including internal IT departments, external service providers, and shared service units. Each provider type may require a distinct strategy.

- **Significance**: Understanding the provider type and aligning the strategy accordingly helps organizations optimize their approach to service delivery, whether it involves insourcing, outsourcing, or a combination of both.

6. Financial Management for IT Services:

- **Principle**: ITIL Service Strategy emphasizes the importance of financial management for IT services. This involves budgeting, accounting, and cost allocation for IT services.

- **Significance**: Effective financial management ensures that IT services are cost-effective, financially transparent, and aligned with the organization's financial goals.

7. Risk Management:

- **Principle**: Service Strategy recognizes that risk is inherent in IT service delivery. Organizations should identify, assess, and manage risks to ensure service continuity and business resilience.

- **Significance**: Proactive risk management helps organizations avoid service disruptions and minimize the impact of unforeseen events.

8. Service Lifecycle Approach:

- **Principle**: Service Strategy is part of the broader ITIL service lifecycle, which includes Service Design, Service Transition, Service Operation, and Continual Service Improvement (CSI). It emphasizes that the strategy should align with and guide activities in all lifecycle stages.

- **Significance**: A holistic service lifecycle approach ensures that strategy is not a one-time endeavor but an ongoing process that supports service delivery throughout the service's lifecycle.

In conclusion, the Service Strategy principles in ITIL provide a solid foundation for organizations to design, develop, and execute their IT service strategies effectively. By adhering to these principles, organizations can ensure that their IT services are value-driven, strategically aligned, financially responsible, and capable of meeting the dynamic needs of both customers and the business.

B. Service Portfolio Management in ITIL: Navigating the Value-Oriented Service Landscape

Service Portfolio Management (SPM) is a crucial component of ITIL (Information Technology Infrastructure Library) Service

Strategy, the phase that forms the strategic backbone of effective IT Service Management (ITSM). SPM serves as the compass that helps organizations steer their service offerings, investments, and decisions toward value-driven outcomes. In this comprehensive exploration, we'll delve into the world of Service Portfolio Management to understand its significance, principles, processes, and benefits.

What Is Service Portfolio Management?

Service Portfolio Management is the process of managing an organization's portfolio of services from inception through development, operation, and eventual retirement. It involves making strategic decisions about which services to invest in, which to maintain, and which to retire based on the organization's objectives, customer needs, and available resources.

Key Principles of Service Portfolio Management:

1. **Value-Centric Approach**:

   - **Principle**: SPM revolves around creating value for both the organization and its customers. Value is at the core of every decision related to services.

   - **Significance**: By focusing on value, organizations can ensure that their service offerings are not just technical solutions but valuable assets that contribute to business objectives and customer satisfaction.

2. **Service Pipeline, Service Catalog, and Retired Services**:

   - **Principle**: The service portfolio consists of three parts: the service pipeline (services in development), the service catalog (live services), and retired services (services that have been retired).

   - **Significance**: This categorization helps organizations visualize their services at different stages of the lifecycle, enabling informed decisions about investment, maintenance, or retirement.

3. **Alignment with Business Objectives**:

   - **Principle**: All services in the portfolio should align with the organization's strategic objectives. Services should be evaluated based on their contribution to these objectives.

   - **Significance**: Alignment ensures that resources are directed toward services that support the organization's goals, optimizing investment and resource allocation.

4. **Continual Service Improvement (CSI)**:

   - **Principle**: SPM is closely tied to Continual Service Improvement (CSI). Ongoing evaluation and improvement of services and the portfolio are fundamental.

- **Significance**: CSI ensures that the service portfolio remains responsive to changing customer needs, technological advancements, and market dynamics.

Processes in Service Portfolio Management:

1. **Define the Service Portfolio**:

   - **Process**: This process involves defining the services that are candidates for inclusion in the portfolio. It includes gathering service ideas, creating business cases, and prioritizing services based on strategic objectives.

2. **Analyze and Approve Services**:

   - **Process**: In this process, services are evaluated in detail, considering their feasibility, cost, expected benefits, and alignment with business objectives. Services that align with the organization's strategy are approved for development.

3. **Charter Services**:

   - **Process**: Approved services are chartered, which means they are formally initiated, and resources are allocated for development.

4. **Monitor and Review Services**:

- **Process**: Services in the portfolio are continuously monitored to assess their performance, customer satisfaction, and alignment with strategic goals. Regular reviews lead to informed decisions about maintaining, enhancing, or retiring services.

Benefits of Effective Service Portfolio Management:

1. **Strategic Alignment**: SPM ensures that services are in line with the organization's strategic objectives, enhancing the organization's overall alignment with business goals.

2. **Resource Optimization**: It helps organizations allocate resources efficiently, ensuring that investments in services deliver maximum value.

3. **Risk Mitigation**: SPM identifies and manages risks associated with services, reducing the likelihood of unexpected disruptions or failures.

4. **Customer Satisfaction**: By focusing on value creation, SPM enhances customer satisfaction and loyalty.

5. **Informed Decision-Making**: It provides a structured approach to making informed decisions about service

investments, maintenance, and retirements.

In conclusion, Service Portfolio Management in ITIL Service Strategy serves as the bridge between an organization's strategic goals and its service offerings. By adhering to the principles and processes of SPM, organizations can navigate the dynamic service landscape with confidence, ensuring that their services remain value-driven, strategically aligned, and responsive to evolving customer needs and market dynamics.

C. Financial Management for IT Services (ITIL): Navigating the Fiscal Waters of IT Service Management

Financial Management for IT Services (FMITS) is a critical process within the ITIL (Information Technology Infrastructure Library) framework, particularly in the Service Strategy phase. It serves as the financial compass that guides organizations in allocating resources, budgeting for IT services, and ensuring cost-effectiveness. In this in-depth exploration, we'll dive into the world of Financial Management for IT Services to understand its significance, objectives, processes, and benefits.

What Is Financial Management for IT Services (FMITS)?

FMITS is the practice of planning and managing the budget and costs associated with IT services. It encompasses activities related to budgeting, accounting, cost allocation, and financial planning. The primary goal of FMITS is to ensure that IT services are financially transparent, cost-effective, and aligned with the organization's financial objectives.

Key Objectives of Financial Management for IT Services:

1. **Cost Transparency**:

    - **Objective**: To provide transparency into the costs associated with IT services, ensuring that both the service provider and customers understand the financial implications of IT service delivery.

    - **Significance**: Cost transparency enables informed decision-making, budget management, and cost control.

2. **Cost Efficiency**:

    - **Objective**: To optimize the use of financial resources by identifying cost-effective ways to deliver IT services without compromising quality.

    - **Significance**: Cost efficiency maximizes the value derived from IT investments and reduces unnecessary expenditures.

3. **Budget Planning and Control**:

- **Objective**: To plan, allocate, and control budgets for IT services, ensuring that financial resources are used effectively and in alignment with business goals.

- **Significance**: Effective budget planning prevents overspending, budget constraints, and financial mismanagement.

4. **Chargeback and Cost Recovery**:

- **Objective**: To implement mechanisms for charging back the costs of IT services to the relevant business units or customers, where applicable.

- **Significance**: Chargeback and cost recovery ensure that the costs of IT services are distributed fairly and that those benefiting from the services bear their share of the expenses.

Processes in Financial Management for IT Services:

1. **Budgeting**:

- **Process**: The budgeting process involves estimating the financial resources required to deliver IT services and creating a budget plan. This plan includes income (revenue) and expenses (costs) related to IT services.

2. **Accounting**:

- **Process**: Accounting focuses on tracking and recording financial transactions related to IT services. It includes maintaining financial records, financial reporting, and ensuring compliance with financial regulations.

3. **Charging**:

- **Process**: Charging involves determining the costs of IT services and establishing a mechanism for billing or charging customers or business units for their usage of IT services.

4. **Costing**:

- **Process**: Costing is the process of assigning and allocating costs to specific IT services or service components. It helps in understanding the cost breakdown of services.

5. **Financial Planning**:

- **Process**: Financial planning encompasses long-term financial planning and forecasting. It helps in aligning financial resources with strategic objectives and accommodating future growth or changes in demand.

Benefits of Effective Financial Management for IT Services:

1. **Cost Control**: FMITS enables organizations to control and manage costs effectively, preventing overspending and financial waste.

2. **Resource Optimization**: It helps organizations allocate financial resources where they are needed most, optimizing resource utilization.

3. **Transparency**: Cost transparency enhances decision-making by providing clear insights into the financial implications of IT services.

4. **Budget Alignment**: FMITS ensures that the budget for IT services aligns with the organization's strategic objectives and business needs.

5. **Compliance**: Proper financial management ensures compliance with financial regulations and standards.

6. **Chargeback Accuracy**: Accurate chargeback mechanisms ensure that the costs of IT services are fairly distributed among stakeholders.

In conclusion, Financial Management for IT Services (FMITS) is a fundamental practice within ITIL that plays a pivotal role in ensuring that IT services are financially transparent, cost-effective, and aligned with organizational objectives. By adhering to the principles and processes of FMITS, organizations can navigate the fiscal waters of IT Service Management with confidence, making informed financial decisions that support business success.

D. Demand Management in ITIL: Meeting Customer Needs with Precision

Demand Management is a crucial process within the ITIL (Information Technology Infrastructure Library) framework, primarily located in the Service Strategy phase. It serves as the bridge between an organization's service offerings and customer requirements. Demand Management helps organizations understand, anticipate, and influence the demand for IT services, ensuring that resources are efficiently allocated to meet customer needs. In this comprehensive exploration, we'll delve into the world of Demand Management to understand its significance, objectives, processes, and benefits.

What Is Demand Management in ITIL?

Demand Management is the practice of understanding, influencing, and aligning IT service demand with an organization's strategic objectives and available resources. It encompasses activities related to forecasting, analyzing, and managing customer demands for IT services. The primary goal of

Demand Management is to ensure that IT services are delivered efficiently, effectively, and in a way that maximizes value for both the organization and its customers.

Key Objectives of Demand Management:

1. **Understanding Customer Needs**:

   - **Objective**: To gain a deep understanding of customer needs, expectations, and requirements for IT services.

   - **Significance**: Understanding customer needs is essential for tailoring IT services to meet those needs effectively.

2. **Demand Forecasting**:

   - **Objective**: To forecast and predict future demand for IT services based on historical data, trends, and changes in the business environment.

   - **Significance**: Accurate demand forecasting helps organizations allocate resources and capacity to meet future service demand.

3. **Influence and Shaping Demand**:

   - **Objective**: To influence and shape customer demand for IT services by promoting and guiding the use of services that align with organizational objectives.

- **Significance**: Shaping demand ensures that resources are focused on services that deliver the most value and align with strategic goals.

4. **Capacity Management Alignment**:

   - **Objective**: To ensure that the capacity of IT services aligns with the demand for those services.

   - **Significance**: Alignment between capacity and demand ensures that services are neither over-provisioned nor under-provisioned, optimizing resource utilization.

Processes in Demand Management:

1. **Demand Forecasting**:

   - **Process**: Demand forecasting involves analyzing historical data, trends, and external factors to predict future demand for IT services.

2. **Demand Influencing**:

   - **Process**: Demand influencing focuses on promoting and guiding customers to use IT services that align with organizational objectives and resource availability.

3. **Demand Shaping**:

   - **Process**: Demand shaping involves actively steering customers toward preferred service options, often through incentives, education, or marketing efforts.

Benefits of Effective Demand Management:

1. **Resource Optimization**: Effective Demand Management ensures that resources are allocated efficiently, preventing overuse or underuse of IT services.

2. **Cost Reduction**: By aligning demand with available resources, organizations can reduce unnecessary costs and optimize their IT budgets.

3. **Customer Satisfaction**: Meeting customer needs and expectations leads to higher customer satisfaction and loyalty.

4. **Strategic Alignment**: Demand Management helps ensure that customer demand aligns with the organization's strategic objectives.

5. **Improved Service Quality**: By focusing on delivering the right services to the right customers at the right time, Demand Management enhances service quality.

6. **Capacity Optimization**: Aligning demand with capacity ensures that services are delivered with optimal performance

and availability.

In conclusion, Demand Management is a pivotal process within ITIL that facilitates the alignment of IT service demand with organizational goals and resources. By adhering to the principles and processes of Demand Management, organizations can meet customer needs with precision, optimize resource allocation, reduce costs, and enhance overall service quality. This practice ultimately contributes to the success and competitiveness of the organization in the ever-evolving IT landscape.

E. Business Relationship Management (BRM) in ITIL: Fostering Strategic Partnerships for Success

Business Relationship Management (BRM) is a fundamental practice within the ITIL (Information Technology Infrastructure Library) framework, primarily situated in the Service Strategy phase. It serves as the linchpin that connects IT service providers with their business counterparts, facilitating collaboration, understanding, and alignment with organizational goals. BRM is instrumental in building strategic partnerships that drive business success. In this comprehensive exploration, we'll delve into the world of Business Relationship Management to understand its significance, objectives, processes, and benefits.

What Is Business Relationship Management (BRM) in ITIL?

Business Relationship Management is the practice of establishing, maintaining, and nurturing relationships between IT service providers and their business partners, including customers, stakeholders, and other business units. BRM focuses on understanding business needs, facilitating communication, and aligning IT services with those needs. Its primary goal is to ensure that IT services are delivered in a way that supports the organization's strategic objectives and adds value to the business.

Key Objectives of Business Relationship Management:

1. **Customer Understanding**:

   - **Objective**: To gain a deep understanding of the business, its goals, challenges, and needs.

   - **Significance**: Understanding the customer's perspective is essential for tailoring IT services to meet their specific requirements.

2. **Alignment with Business Objectives**:

   - **Objective**: To align IT services, strategies, and resources with the organization's strategic goals.

   - **Significance**: Alignment ensures that IT investments

and activities contribute directly to business success.

3. **Effective Communication**:

- **Objective**: To facilitate clear and effective communication between IT and business stakeholders.

- **Significance**: Effective communication ensures that IT services are responsive to changing business needs and expectations.

4. **Value Delivery**:

- **Objective**: To ensure that IT services provide measurable value to the organization and its customers.

- **Significance**: Value delivery is a key measure of IT's contribution to business success.

Processes in Business Relationship Management:

1. **Identify and Classify Stakeholders**:

- **Process**: Identifying and classifying stakeholders involves identifying the individuals and groups that have an interest in IT services and classifying them based on their level of influence and importance.

2. **Engage with Stakeholders**:

   - **Process**: Engaging with stakeholders involves actively communicating with them, understanding their needs and concerns, and maintaining ongoing relationships.

3. **Understand Business Needs and Objectives**:

   - **Process**: Understanding business needs and objectives entails conducting regular discussions and assessments to gain insights into the business's strategic goals and challenges.

4. **Define Service Requirements**:

   - **Process**: Defining service requirements involves documenting and translating business needs into specific IT service requirements and capabilities.

5. **Service Level Management (SLM)**:

   - **Process**: SLM is closely related to BRM and focuses on defining, measuring, and reporting on service levels and performance in alignment with business requirements.

Benefits of Effective Business Relationship Management:

1. **Strategic Alignment**: BRM ensures that IT services are closely aligned with the organization's strategic objectives,

enhancing overall alignment.

2. **Customer Satisfaction**: By understanding and meeting customer needs, BRM enhances customer satisfaction and loyalty.

3. **Clear Communication**: Effective communication between IT and business stakeholders reduces misunderstandings and promotes collaboration.

4. **Value Demonstration**: BRM helps IT demonstrate the value it provides to the business, contributing to a positive perception of IT's role.

5. **Proactive Problem Solving**: BRM facilitates proactive problem-solving by addressing business challenges and needs before they become critical issues.

6. **Improved Decision-Making**: Informed by a deeper understanding of the business, BRM supports data-driven decision-making.

In conclusion, Business Relationship Management is a pivotal practice within ITIL that fosters collaboration, understanding, and alignment between IT and the business. By adhering to the principles and processes of BRM, organizations can build strategic partnerships that drive business success, enhance customer satisfaction, and ensure that IT services are delivered in a way that adds measurable value to the organization.

CHAPTER 4

ITIL Service Design

Within the realm of IT Service Management (ITSM), crafting services that excel in quality, efficiency, and alignment with organizational goals is a strategic imperative. ITIL Service Design stands at the forefront of this mission, serving as the architect's table where IT services are meticulously planned, designed, and prepared for implementation. In this introductory exploration of ITIL Service Design, we embark on a journey to understand its significance, objectives, and the role it plays in sculpting IT services that not only meet but exceed expectations. Join us as we unveil the art and science of designing services for excellence in ITSM.

A. Service Design Principles in ITIL: The Pillars of Effective IT Service Blueprinting

Service Design is a crucial phase within the ITIL (Information Technology Infrastructure Library) framework, where the foundation is laid for delivering IT services that align seamlessly with business needs and objectives. Service Design principles serve as the guiding pillars for crafting IT services that excel in quality, efficiency, and value. In this in-depth exploration, we'll delve into these critical Service Design principles that underpin the process of blueprinting services for success:

1. Design for the Customer Experience:

- **Principle**: The customer experience is paramount in Service Design. Services should be designed with a focus on meeting and exceeding customer expectations.

- **Significance**: Designing for the customer experience ensures that services are user-friendly, accessible, and capable of delivering the desired outcomes.

2. Start with the Business Objectives:

- **Principle**: Service Design should begin by understanding and aligning with the business objectives and requirements. Services must support and contribute to these objectives.

- **Significance**: Aligning with business objectives ensures that IT services are strategically relevant and have a clear purpose in the organization.

3. Design for Scalability and Flexibility:

- **Principle**: IT services should be designed with scalability and flexibility in mind to accommodate changing demands and requirements.

- **Significance**: Scalable and flexible services can adapt to evolving business needs, preventing service disruptions and costly re-designs.

4. Standardization and Reusability:

- **Principle**: Promote standardization and reusability of components and processes to streamline service design and reduce complexity.

- **Significance**: Standardization and reusability enhance efficiency, consistency, and ease of maintenance in service delivery.

5. Continual Improvement as a Design Objective:

- **Principle**: Design services with built-in mechanisms for continual improvement. Monitor, measure, and analyze service performance to identify areas for enhancement.

- **Significance**: Continual improvement ensures that services remain aligned with business needs and deliver increasing value over time.

6. Security and Risk Management:

- **Principle**: Incorporate security and risk management into service design to safeguard against potential threats and vulnerabilities.

- **Significance**: Proactive security measures protect both the service provider and customers, minimizing risks and disruptions.

7. Service Ownership and Accountability:

- **Principle**: Clearly define service ownership and accountability. Assign responsibilities for the design, delivery, and support of each service.

- **Significance**: Accountability ensures that services are managed effectively, with clear lines of responsibility and authority.

8. Design for Manageability and Monitoring:

- **Principle**: Design services with manageability and monitoring in mind. Implement tools and processes for monitoring service performance and health.

- **Significance**: Manageable services are easier to operate and maintain, leading to improved reliability and availability.

9. Cost-Effective Service Design:

- **Principle**: Strive for cost-effective service design by optimizing resource utilization, reducing waste, and aligning with budget constraints.

- **Significance**: Cost-effective design helps maximize the return on investment in IT services.

10. Service Transition Considerations:

- **Principle**: Service Design should consider the requirements and readiness for transitioning services into live operation (Service Transition phase).

- **Significance**: A smooth transition minimizes service disruptions and ensures that services are ready to meet customer needs.

In conclusion, Service Design principles in ITIL provide a solid foundation for organizations to create IT services that align with business objectives, deliver exceptional customer experiences, and adapt to changing demands. By adhering to these principles, organizations can craft services that are not only efficient and reliable but also strategic assets that contribute to the overall success of the business.

B. Service Catalog Management in ITIL: Orchestrating Service Excellence

Service Catalog Management is a pivotal process within the ITIL (Information Technology Infrastructure Library) framework, primarily situated in the Service Design phase. It serves as the curator and orchestrator of IT services, offering a structured and accessible catalog of services to customers, business stakeholders, and IT teams. Service Catalog Management plays a crucial role in aligning IT services with business needs and providing transparency in service offerings. In this comprehensive exploration, we'll delve into the world of Service Catalog Management to understand its significance, objectives, processes, and benefits.

What Is Service Catalog Management in ITIL?

Service Catalog Management is the practice of creating, maintaining, and making available a catalog of IT services offered by an organization. This catalog serves as a comprehensive and user-friendly repository of services, their descriptions, service levels, costs, and other relevant information. The primary goal of Service Catalog Management is to ensure that IT services are clearly defined, accessible, and aligned with the organization's business objectives.

Key Objectives of Service Catalog Management:

1. **Service Clarity and Transparency**:

    -   **Objective**: To provide clarity and transparency regarding available IT services, their features, service levels, and associated costs.

    -   **Significance**: Clarity and transparency help customers and stakeholders make informed decisions about selecting and using IT services.

2. **Alignment with Business Needs**:

- **Objective**: To ensure that IT services in the catalog are closely aligned with the current and future needs of the business.

- **Significance**: Alignment with business needs ensures that IT services support the organization's strategic goals.

3. **Service Level Agreements (SLAs) and Expectations**:

- **Objective**: To define and communicate service levels, SLAs, and expectations associated with each service listed in the catalog.

- **Significance**: Clear SLAs and expectations help manage customer and stakeholder expectations and ensure service delivery in line with commitments.

4. **Promotion of Standard Services**:

- **Objective**: To promote and encourage the use of standard services listed in the catalog to reduce customization and complexity.

- **Significance**: Standard services are typically more efficient and cost-effective to deliver.

Processes in Service Catalog Management:

1. **Define Service Catalog**:

   - **Process**: Define the scope and content of the service catalog, including the services to be included, their descriptions, service levels, and costs.

2. **Create and Maintain Service Catalog Entries**:

   - **Process**: Create, update, and maintain entries for each IT service, ensuring that the catalog remains accurate and up to date.

3. **Publish and Distribute Service Catalog**:

   - **Process**: Make the service catalog accessible to customers, business stakeholders, and IT teams through appropriate channels, such as a web portal or documentation.

4. **Review and Update Service Catalog**:

   - **Process**: Regularly review and update the service catalog to reflect changes in services, service levels, or customer needs.

Benefits of Effective Service Catalog Management:

1. **Enhanced Customer Experience**: A well-managed service

catalog provides customers with a clear view of available services, improving their experience.

2. **Service Alignment**: It ensures that services are closely aligned with business needs, contributing to business objectives.

3. **Increased Efficiency**: Promoting standard services reduces the complexity of service delivery, leading to increased efficiency.

4. **Transparency**: Service Catalog Management provides transparency into service offerings, service levels, and costs, reducing confusion and disputes.

5. **Effective Service Level Management**: Clear SLAs and expectations enable effective Service Level Management, ensuring that services meet agreed-upon standards.

6. **Cost Control**: Understanding service costs helps organizations manage and control their IT budgets effectively.

In conclusion, Service Catalog Management is an essential practice within ITIL that helps organizations provide clarity, transparency, and alignment in their IT service offerings. By adhering to the principles and processes of Service Catalog Management, organizations can deliver IT services that meet customer needs, support business objectives, and promote efficiency and cost-effectiveness in service delivery.

C. Service Level Management (SLM) in ITIL: Crafting Agreements for Exceptional Service Quality

Service Level Management (SLM) is a pivotal process within the ITIL (Information Technology Infrastructure Library) framework, primarily situated in the Service Design phase. It serves as the conductor of service quality, responsible for defining, negotiating, and monitoring Service Level Agreements (SLAs) between IT service providers and their customers. SLM plays a crucial role in ensuring that IT services meet or exceed customer expectations, delivering value and aligning with business objectives. In this comprehensive exploration, we'll delve into the world of Service Level Management to understand its significance, objectives, processes, and benefits.

What Is Service Level Management (SLM) in ITIL?

Service Level Management is the practice of defining, negotiating, and managing Service Level Agreements (SLAs) between IT service providers and their customers or stakeholders. SLAs are formal agreements that outline the expectations, responsibilities, and metrics for service delivery. The primary goal of SLM is to ensure that IT services are delivered in a way that meets or exceeds the agreed-upon service levels and contributes to customer satisfaction and business success.

Key Objectives of Service Level Management:

1. **Define Clear Service Expectations**:

   - **Objective**: To define and document clear and measurable service expectations in the form of SLAs.

   - **Significance**: Clear expectations help manage customer and stakeholder perceptions and ensure that services align with business needs.

2. **Alignment with Business Objectives**:

   - **Objective**: To ensure that SLAs are aligned with the organization's strategic objectives and contribute to business success.

   - **Significance**: Alignment with business objectives ensures that IT services support the organization's overall goals.

3. **Negotiate and Agree on SLAs**:

   - **Objective**: To negotiate and agree upon SLAs with customers or stakeholders, considering their requirements and the organization's capabilities.

   - **Significance**: Agreement on SLAs sets clear boundaries and commitments for both parties, promoting a shared understanding.

4. **Monitor and Report on Service Performance**:

- **Objective**: To monitor service performance against SLAs, report on deviations, and take corrective actions when necessary.

- **Significance**: Monitoring and reporting ensure that services are delivered in line with commitments and help identify areas for improvement.

5. **Continuous Improvement**:

- **Objective**: To continually review and improve SLAs and service levels based on changing business needs and customer feedback.

- **Significance**: Continuous improvement ensures that services remain responsive to evolving requirements.

Processes in Service Level Management:

1. **Define Service Level Requirements**:

- **Process**: Define the service level requirements for each IT service, considering customer and stakeholder needs and expectations.

2. **Negotiate and Agree on SLAs**:

- **Process**: Engage in negotiations with customers or

stakeholders to agree upon SLAs, documenting the terms, conditions, and responsibilities.

3. **Monitor and Report on Service Performance**:

    - **Process**: Continuously monitor service performance against SLAs, report on deviations or breaches, and take corrective actions as needed.

4. **Review and Improve SLAs**:

    - **Process**: Periodically review and update SLAs based on changing business needs, customer feedback, and service performance data.

Benefits of Effective Service Level Management:

1. **Customer Satisfaction**: SLM ensures that services meet or exceed customer expectations, enhancing customer satisfaction and loyalty.

2. **Alignment with Business Goals**: SLAs are aligned with business objectives, ensuring that IT services support strategic goals.

3. **Transparency and Accountability**: Clear SLAs provide transparency and accountability, reducing misunderstandings and disputes.

4. **Efficient Resource Allocation**: SLM helps allocate resources

effectively to meet service commitments.

5. **Continuous Improvement**: Continuous review and improvement of SLAs lead to service enhancements over time.

6. **Data-Driven Decision-Making**: Monitoring and reporting provide data for informed decision-making and problem resolution.

In conclusion, Service Level Management is a pivotal practice within ITIL that ensures IT services are delivered in a way that meets or exceeds customer expectations, supports business objectives, and contributes to overall service quality. By adhering to the principles and processes of SLM, organizations can create a culture of service excellence, fostering customer satisfaction and long-term success.

D. Capacity Management in ITIL: Optimizing Resources for Peak Performance

Capacity Management is a crucial process within the ITIL (Information Technology Infrastructure Library) framework, primarily situated in the Service Design and Service Operation phases. It serves as the architect and guardian of an organization's IT resources, ensuring that IT services have the capacity and performance capabilities to meet business needs. Capacity Management plays a pivotal role in optimizing resource utilization, preventing bottlenecks, and ensuring IT services run at peak performance. In this comprehensive exploration, we'll delve into the world of Capacity Management to understand its significance, objectives, processes, and benefits.

What Is Capacity Management in ITIL?

Capacity Management is the practice of proactively planning, monitoring, and managing the IT resources required to support current and future business needs. These resources can include hardware, software, network infrastructure, storage, and more. The primary goal of Capacity Management is to ensure that IT services have the capacity to deliver the required performance levels, maintaining service quality and meeting customer expectations.

Key Objectives of Capacity Management:

1. **Resource Optimization**:

   - **Objective**: To optimize the use of IT resources, ensuring that they are used efficiently and cost-effectively.

   - **Significance**: Resource optimization prevents over-provisioning (wasting resources) and under-provisioning (insufficient resources).

2. **Performance Management**:

- **Objective**: To monitor and manage the performance of IT services to meet or exceed agreed-upon service levels.

- **Significance**: Performance management ensures that services run smoothly and deliver a consistent user experience.

3. **Capacity Planning**:

- **Objective**: To predict future capacity requirements based on business growth and technology trends.

- **Significance**: Capacity planning ensures that IT resources are available when needed, preventing service disruptions.

4. **Cost Control**:

- **Objective**: To control and optimize the costs associated with IT resources and capacity.

- **Significance**: Cost control helps organizations manage IT budgets effectively and allocate resources where they are needed most.

Processes in Capacity Management:

1. **Business Capacity Management**:

   - **Process**: Focuses on aligning IT capacity with business requirements and objectives. It involves understanding business needs and translating them into IT resource requirements.

2. **Service Capacity Management**:

   - **Process**: Concentrates on managing the capacity and performance of individual IT services. It ensures that services have the necessary resources to meet their performance targets.

3. **Component Capacity Management**:

   - **Process**: Focuses on the capacity and performance of individual IT components, such as servers, networks, and storage. It involves monitoring and managing the utilization of these components.

4. **Capacity Planning**:

   - **Process**: Involves forecasting future capacity requirements based on historical data, business growth projections, and technology trends. Capacity planning helps organizations prepare for future resource needs.

5. **Performance Management**:

- **Process**: Monitors the performance of IT services and components, identifies performance bottlenecks, and takes corrective actions to optimize performance.

Benefits of Effective Capacity Management:

1. **Resource Optimization**: Capacity Management ensures that IT resources are used efficiently, minimizing waste and reducing costs.

2. **Improved Performance**: By optimizing capacity and managing performance, IT services consistently meet or exceed service levels.

3. **Proactive Problem Resolution**: Capacity Management identifies and addresses performance bottlenecks before they impact service quality.

4. **Cost Control**: Efficient capacity planning and resource optimization contribute to effective IT budget management.

5. **Scalability**: Capacity planning allows organizations to scale resources up or down as needed to support business growth or changes.

6. **Enhanced Reliability**: By preventing resource shortages, Capacity Management enhances the reliability and availability

of IT services.

In conclusion, Capacity Management is a fundamental practice within ITIL that ensures IT services have the capacity and performance capabilities to meet business needs efficiently and cost-effectively. By adhering to the principles and processes of Capacity Management, organizations can optimize resource utilization, prevent performance issues, and maintain peak performance, ultimately contributing to the success and competitiveness of the organization.

E. Availability Management in ITIL: Ensuring IT Services are Always Ready

Availability Management is a critical process within the ITIL (Information Technology Infrastructure Library) framework, primarily situated in the Service Design and Service Operation phases. It serves as the guardian of IT services' availability, ensuring that they are consistently accessible and reliable to meet business needs. Availability Management plays a pivotal role in minimizing service disruptions, enhancing resilience, and safeguarding IT services against downtime. In this comprehensive exploration, we'll delve into the world of Availability Management to understand its significance, objectives, processes, and benefits.

What Is Availability Management in ITIL?

Availability Management is the practice of planning, monitoring, measuring, and optimizing the availability of IT services. Availability refers to the ability of an IT service to perform its functions when required, without interruption or degradation in performance. The primary goal of Availability Management is to ensure that IT services meet agreed-upon availability targets, aligning with business requirements and Service Level Agreements (SLAs).

Key Objectives of Availability Management:

1. **Service Availability Optimization**:

   - **Objective**: To optimize the availability of IT services to meet or exceed agreed-upon targets and customer expectations.

   - **Significance**: Service availability is critical to ensuring that IT services are consistently accessible and reliable.

2. **Risk Management**:

   - **Objective**: To identify and mitigate risks that could impact the availability of IT services, including proactive measures to prevent incidents.

- **Significance**: Risk management helps prevent service disruptions and minimize their impact when they occur.

3. **Resilience Enhancement**:

   - **Objective**: To enhance the resilience of IT services, ensuring that they can recover quickly from incidents and disruptions.

   - **Significance**: Resilient services minimize downtime and service unavailability.

4. **Monitoring and Reporting**:

   - **Objective**: To continually monitor service availability, measure performance, and report on availability metrics.

   - **Significance**: Monitoring and reporting enable proactive management of availability and identification of areas for improvement.

Processes in Availability Management:

1. **Availability Management Information System (AMIS)**:

   - **Process**: Establishes and maintains an information system that supports Availability Management activities, including data collection, analysis, and reporting.

2. **Availability Planning**:

   - **Process**: Develops plans to optimize service availability, including defining availability targets and designing service resilience.

3. **Availability Monitoring and Measurement**:

   - **Process**: Monitors and measures the availability of IT services against agreed-upon targets and reports on performance.

4. **Availability Assessment**:

   - **Process**: Conducts regular assessments to identify risks to service availability, including vulnerabilities and potential incidents.

5. **Risk Management**:

   - **Process**: Identifies, assesses, and manages risks to service availability, implementing preventive measures where necessary.

6. **Availability Improvement**:

   - **Process**: Drives continuous improvement in service availability by implementing changes and enhancements based on monitoring and assessment data.

Benefits of Effective Availability Management:

1. **Service Reliability**: Effective Availability Management ensures that IT services are reliable and consistently accessible.

2. **Reduced Downtime**: Proactive risk management and resilience enhancement minimize service downtime and disruptions.

3. **Enhanced Business Continuity**: Availability Management contributes to business continuity by ensuring that critical IT services are available during disruptions.

4. **Improved Customer Satisfaction**: Reliable services lead to higher customer satisfaction and confidence.

5. **Optimized Resource Utilization**: Resource allocation is optimized to ensure that services meet availability targets without over-provisioning.

6. **Cost Control**: Managing availability effectively helps control costs associated with service disruptions and downtime.

In conclusion, Availability Management is a crucial practice within ITIL that ensures IT services are consistently available and reliable to meet business needs. By adhering to the principles and processes of Availability Management, organizations can minimize service disruptions, enhance resilience, and safeguard the availability of IT services, ultimately contributing to the success and competitiveness of the organization.

F. IT Service Continuity Management (ITSCM) in ITIL: Safeguarding Business Resilience

IT Service Continuity Management (ITSCM) is a vital process within the ITIL (Information Technology Infrastructure Library) framework, primarily situated in the Service Design phase. It serves as the guardian of an organization's ability to continue delivering critical IT services in the face of disruptions or disasters. ITSCM is responsible for planning, implementing, and maintaining measures that ensure IT services can be restored and resumed promptly in adverse situations. In this comprehensive exploration, we'll delve into the world of IT Service Continuity Management to understand its significance, objectives, processes, and benefits.

What Is IT Service Continuity Management (ITSCM) in ITIL?

IT Service Continuity Management (ITSCM) is the practice of planning, designing, implementing, and maintaining measures that ensure IT services can continue or be rapidly restored in the event of a disruption or disaster. The goal of ITSCM is to minimize the impact of disruptions on the organization's ability to deliver critical IT services, protecting business operations and customer satisfaction.

Key Objectives of IT Service Continuity Management:

1. **Risk Assessment and Mitigation**:

   - **Objective**: To identify potential risks and vulnerabilities that could disrupt IT services and implement measures to mitigate these risks.

   - **Significance**: Risk assessment helps prevent service disruptions and minimizes their impact when they occur.

2. **Service Recovery Planning**:

   - **Objective**: To develop comprehensive recovery plans that outline the steps and procedures for restoring IT services to operational status.

   - **Significance**: Recovery plans ensure that IT services can be quickly and effectively restored, minimizing downtime.

3. **Testing and Validation**:

   - **Objective**: To regularly test and validate the effectiveness of IT service recovery plans and measures.

   - **Significance**: Testing ensures that recovery plans work as intended and identifies areas for improvement.

4. **Documentation and Communication**:

   - **Objective**: To maintain up-to-date documentation of recovery plans, responsibilities, and communication procedures.

   - **Significance**: Clear documentation and communication are essential during disruptions to coordinate response efforts.

Processes in IT Service Continuity Management:

1. **Initiation and Requirements Definition**:

   - **Process**: Begins by defining the scope and requirements of ITSCM, identifying critical services, and setting recovery objectives.

2. **Risk Assessment and Management**:

   - **Process**: Identifies risks to IT services, assesses their impact, and implements risk mitigation measures.

3. **Business Impact Analysis (BIA)**:

   - **Process**: Analyzes the impact of service disruptions on business operations and identifies recovery priorities.

4. **Strategy and Plan Development**:

   - **Process**: Develops ITSCM strategies, recovery plans, and associated documentation for critical services.

5. **Implementation of Recovery Plans**:

   - **Process**: Puts recovery plans into action when disruptions occur, including activating crisis management teams and resources.

6. **Testing and Validation**:

   - **Process**: Regularly tests recovery plans and measures to ensure they are effective and can be executed successfully.

7. **Ongoing Maintenance and Review**:

   - **Process**: Continuously reviews and updates ITSCM plans, considering changes in technology, business needs, and risks.

Benefits of Effective IT Service Continuity Management:

1. **Business Resilience**: ITSCM ensures that critical IT services are resilient, enabling the organization to withstand disruptions and continue operations.

2. **Minimized Downtime**: Effective recovery plans and testing minimize downtime and service disruptions, reducing business impact.

3. **Risk Reduction**: Identifying and mitigating risks reduces the likelihood and severity of service disruptions.

4. **Customer Confidence**: The ability to maintain critical services during disruptions enhances customer confidence and trust.

5. **Legal and Regulatory Compliance**: ITSCM helps organizations meet legal and regulatory requirements for business continuity.

6. **Cost Savings**: Minimizing service disruptions and downtime reduces the financial impact of IT incidents.

In conclusion, IT Service Continuity Management is a crucial practice within ITIL that ensures IT services can continue or be rapidly restored in the face of disruptions or disasters. By adhering to the principles and processes of ITSCM, organizations can protect business operations, maintain customer satisfaction, and demonstrate resilience in the face of adversity.

CHAPTER 5

ITIL Service Transition

ITIL Service Transition is a pivotal phase within the ITIL (Information Technology Infrastructure Library) framework, marking the critical juncture where new or modified IT services take their first steps from development to live operation. This phase focuses on ensuring a smooth and controlled transition of services into the operational environment. It encompasses processes and activities that are essential for minimizing risks, managing changes, and ensuring that services are ready to deliver value to customers and the business as a whole.

In this introductory exploration of ITIL Service Transition, we embark on a journey to understand its significance, objectives, and the pivotal role it plays in orchestrating the evolution of IT services. Join us as we unravel the intricacies of this phase, where innovation meets execution, and IT services come to life in the service of organizational goals and customer needs.

A. Service Transition Principles in ITIL: Navigating the Waters of Change

Service Transition is a critical phase within the ITIL

(Information Technology Infrastructure Library) framework, where new or modified IT services transition from development to live operation. The principles that underpin Service Transition are foundational to ensuring that this phase is executed efficiently, with minimal disruption to business operations and a focus on delivering value to customers. In this in-depth exploration, we'll delve into these crucial Service Transition principles and their significance in orchestrating successful service changes.

1. Service Transition Is a Controlled Process:

- **Principle**: Service Transition should be a controlled and organized process with defined stages and checkpoints.

- **Significance**: Control ensures that changes are carefully planned, assessed, and executed, minimizing the risk of service disruptions and unexpected consequences.

2. Change Is Inevitable; Prepare for It:

- **Principle**: Change is a constant in IT, and Service Transition acknowledges this inevitability by providing structured processes for managing it.

- **Significance**: Preparedness allows organizations to handle changes effectively, adapt to evolving needs, and stay competitive.

3. Consistency and Repeatability Are Key:

- **Principle**: Service Transition processes should be consistent and repeatable, ensuring that changes are managed uniformly and reliably.

- **Significance**: Consistency reduces the likelihood of errors and helps maintain service quality.

4. Collaboration Across Stakeholders:

- **Principle**: Effective collaboration among various stakeholders, including development, operations, and business teams, is essential.

- **Significance**: Collaboration ensures that everyone is aligned with the goals of the service change, promoting a smooth transition.

5. Testing Is Crucial:

- **Principle**: Rigorous testing of new or modified services, including integration, performance, and user acceptance testing, is essential.

- **Significance**: Testing identifies issues before services go live, reducing the risk of service disruptions and customer dissatisfaction.

6. Documentation Matters:

- **Principle**: Comprehensive documentation of changes, processes, and procedures is critical for transparency and knowledge sharing.

- **Significance**: Documentation ensures that everyone involved understands the changes and can respond effectively when needed.

7. Minimize Unplanned Service Downtime:

- **Principle**: Service Transition aims to minimize unplanned service downtime during changes.

- **Significance**: Reducing downtime maintains service availability and minimizes disruptions to business operations.

8. Focus on Customer Value:

- **Principle**: The ultimate goal of Service Transition is to deliver value to customers by ensuring that services meet their needs and expectations.

- **Significance**: Customer-centricity drives service excellence and customer satisfaction.

9. Continuous Improvement:

- **Principle**: Service Transition should incorporate feedback and lessons learned into its processes for continual improvement.

- **Significance**: Continuous improvement ensures that the transition process becomes more efficient and effective over time.

10. Change Evaluation:

- **Principle**: Evaluate the success of service changes against predefined criteria and objectives.

- **Significance**: Evaluation provides insights into the impact and effectiveness of changes, guiding future improvements.

In conclusion, Service Transition principles serve as the guiding light for organizations navigating the complex waters of change in the ITIL framework. By adhering to these principles, organizations can ensure that service changes are executed with precision, minimal disruption, and a relentless focus on delivering value to customers and the business.

B. Change Management in ITIL: Navigating the Seas of Transformation

Change Management is a cornerstone process within the ITIL (Information Technology Infrastructure Library) framework, spanning across the Service Transition and Service Operation phases. Its purpose is to ensure that changes to IT services and infrastructure are systematically planned, assessed, approved, implemented, and reviewed. Change Management plays a pivotal role in minimizing risks, maintaining service quality, and facilitating the successful adoption of changes within an organization. In this comprehensive exploration, we'll delve into the world of Change Management to understand its significance, objectives, processes, and benefits.

What Is Change Management in ITIL?

Change Management is the practice of controlling changes to the IT environment, including hardware, software, processes, documentation, and organizational structures. It encompasses everything from minor adjustments to major transformations and ensures that changes are introduced in a way that minimizes disruption and aligns with business objectives. The primary goal of Change Management is to enable beneficial changes while minimizing adverse effects on IT services.

Key Objectives of Change Management:

1. **Risk Mitigation**:

   - **Objective**: To identify potential risks associated with changes and implement measures to mitigate these risks.

   - **Significance**: Risk mitigation reduces the likelihood of service disruptions and unexpected consequences.

2. **Service Continuity**:

- **Objective**: To ensure that changes do not negatively impact the continuity and availability of IT services.

- **Significance**: Maintaining service continuity is essential to meet business needs and customer expectations.

3. **Effective Communication**:

- **Objective**: To facilitate clear communication and coordination among stakeholders during the change process.

- **Significance**: Effective communication minimizes misunderstandings and ensures that everyone is aligned with the change objectives.

4. **Change Prioritization**:

- **Objective**: To prioritize changes based on their impact, urgency, and business value.

- **Significance**: Prioritization ensures that critical changes are addressed promptly and that resources are allocated appropriately.

5. **Continuous Improvement**:

  - **Objective**: To continually evaluate and improve the Change Management process based on feedback and lessons learned.

  - **Significance**: Continuous improvement enhances the effectiveness and efficiency of Change Management.

Processes in Change Management:

1. **Request for Change (RFC)**:

  - **Process**: Initiated when a change is proposed, the RFC process involves documenting and evaluating the change request.

2. **Change Evaluation**:

  - **Process**: Assesses the potential impact and risks of proposed changes, determining whether they should proceed to the next stage.

3. **Change Approval**:

  - **Process**: Involves gaining approval from the Change Advisory Board (CAB) or relevant stakeholders to authorize the change's implementation.

4. **Change Implementation**:

- **Process**: Carries out the change in a controlled and coordinated manner, ensuring that it is performed according to the approved plan.

5. **Review and Closure**:

- **Process**: After the change is implemented, a review is conducted to evaluate its success and gather lessons learned.

Benefits of Effective Change Management:

1. **Risk Reduction**: Change Management identifies and mitigates risks associated with changes, minimizing the likelihood of service disruptions.

2. **Service Continuity**: Changes are introduced without negatively impacting service continuity, ensuring uninterrupted service availability.

3. **Alignment with Business Goals**: Change prioritization aligns changes with business objectives, delivering value to the organization.

4. **Effective Communication**: Clear communication facilitates cooperation and ensures that stakeholders are informed and engaged.

5. **Efficient Resource Allocation**: Prioritization ensures that resources are allocated to address the most critical changes first.

6. **Continuous Improvement**: Ongoing evaluation and improvement enhance the effectiveness and efficiency of Change Management.

In conclusion, Change Management is a foundational practice within ITIL that ensures changes to IT services and infrastructure are introduced systematically, with minimal disruption and maximum alignment with business objectives. By adhering to the principles and processes of Change Management, organizations can navigate the seas of transformation with confidence, embracing change as an opportunity for growth and improvement.

C. Release and Deployment Management in ITIL: Delivering Change with Precision

Release and Deployment Management is a pivotal process within the ITIL (Information Technology Infrastructure Library) framework, primarily situated in the Service Transition phase. This process orchestrates the careful planning, testing, and deployment of new or modified IT services, ensuring they are introduced into the live environment with precision and minimal disruption. Release and Deployment Management play a crucial role in delivering value to customers and the business by making changes available for use. In this comprehensive exploration, we'll delve into the world of Release and Deployment Management to understand its significance, objectives, processes, and benefits.

What Is Release and Deployment Management in ITIL?

Release and Deployment Management is the practice of planning, scheduling, and controlling the build, test, and deployment of new or modified IT services into the live environment. It encompasses everything from deploying software updates to launching entirely new services. The primary goal of Release and Deployment Management is to ensure that changes are introduced with minimal disruption, aligned with business objectives, and delivering value to customers.

Key Objectives of Release and Deployment Management:

1. **Minimize Disruption**:

    - **Objective**: To minimize service disruptions and maintain service availability when introducing changes.

    - **Significance**: Minimizing disruption ensures that business operations continue without interruption.

2. **Efficient Deployment**:

    - **Objective**: To ensure that changes are deployed

efficiently and effectively, with minimal errors or defects.

- **Significance**: Efficient deployment reduces the likelihood of service outages and customer dissatisfaction.

3. **Risk Management**:

- **Objective**: To identify and mitigate risks associated with deploying changes into the live environment.

- **Significance**: Risk mitigation reduces the impact of issues that may arise during deployment.

4. **Verification and Validation**:

- **Objective**: To verify and validate that changes meet the defined specifications and requirements.

- **Significance**: Verification and validation ensure that changes are of high quality and align with business needs.

Processes in Release and Deployment Management:

1. **Release Planning**:

- **Process**: Involves planning the release of changes, including scheduling, resource allocation, and risk assessment.

2. **Release Build and Test**:

   - **Process**: Focuses on building and thoroughly testing the changes, ensuring they meet specifications and quality standards.

3. **Release Deployment**:

   - **Process**: Coordinates the deployment of changes into the live environment, following carefully defined procedures and minimizing disruption.

4. **Early Life Support**:

   - **Process**: Provides support and assistance immediately after the deployment to address any issues that may arise.

5. **Knowledge Management**:

   - **Process**: Ensures that knowledge and information related to the release and deployment are documented and accessible.

Benefits of Effective Release and Deployment Management:

1. **Minimized Disruption**: Effective management reduces the

risk of service disruptions and ensures that changes are introduced smoothly.

2. **Efficient Deployment**: Changes are deployed efficiently, reducing the likelihood of errors and defects.

3. **Risk Reduction**: Risk assessment and mitigation measures minimize the impact of issues during deployment.

4. **Enhanced Service Quality**: Verification and validation ensure that changes meet specified quality standards.

5. **Alignment with Business Goals**: Changes are aligned with business objectives, delivering value to the organization and customers.

6. **Knowledge Sharing**: Knowledge management ensures that information related to releases is documented and accessible for future reference.

In conclusion, Release and Deployment Management is a critical practice within ITIL that ensures changes are introduced into the live environment with precision, minimal disruption, and a relentless focus on delivering value to customers and the business. By adhering to the principles and processes of Release and Deployment Management, organizations can embrace change as an opportunity for growth and innovation while maintaining the stability and continuity of IT services.

D. Knowledge Management in ITIL: Nurturing the Wellspring of Wisdom

Knowledge Management is a fundamental process within the ITIL (Information Technology Infrastructure Library) framework, spanning across multiple phases, including Service Transition, Service Operation, and Continual Service Improvement. This process revolves around the systematic creation, capture, storage, and dissemination of knowledge and information within an organization. Knowledge Management plays a pivotal role in enhancing service quality, improving efficiency, and fostering innovation. In this comprehensive exploration, we'll delve into the world of Knowledge Management to understand its significance, objectives, processes, and benefits.

What Is Knowledge Management in ITIL?

Knowledge Management is the practice of gathering, organizing, and sharing knowledge and information to support the effective delivery and management of IT services. It encompasses the creation and maintenance of a structured knowledge base, best practice repositories, and mechanisms for sharing insights and expertise. The primary goal of Knowledge Management is to ensure that relevant knowledge is readily available to support decision-making, problem-solving, and service improvement.

Key Objectives of Knowledge Management:

1. **Knowledge Capture**:

   - **Objective**: To capture and document knowledge and information from various sources within the organization.

   - **Significance**: Captured knowledge becomes a valuable organizational asset, available for reference and use.

2. **Knowledge Storage and Retrieval**:

   - **Objective**: To establish repositories and mechanisms for storing, organizing, and retrieving knowledge efficiently.

   - **Significance**: Easy access to knowledge enhances decision-making, problem-solving, and service delivery.

3. **Knowledge Sharing**:

   - **Objective**: To facilitate the sharing of knowledge and expertise among staff members and teams.

   - **Significance**: Knowledge sharing fosters collaboration, accelerates learning, and promotes innovation.

4. **Problem Resolution**:

- **Objective**: To use knowledge to resolve incidents and problems quickly and effectively.

- **Significance**: Knowledge-driven problem resolution reduces downtime and improves service quality.

Processes in Knowledge Management:

1. **Knowledge Capture**:

- **Process**: Involves capturing knowledge from various sources, such as experts, documentation, and incident records.

2. **Knowledge Storage and Organization**:

- **Process**: Focuses on structuring and organizing knowledge for easy retrieval and use, often through the creation of a knowledge base.

3. **Knowledge Sharing and Collaboration**:

- **Process**: Facilitates the sharing of knowledge among staff members and teams, promoting collaboration and knowledge exchange.

4. **Knowledge Transfer**:

- **Process**: Ensures that knowledge is transferred to the

right individuals or teams within the organization.

5. **Knowledge Maintenance and Improvement**:

   - **Process**: Regularly reviews and updates knowledge assets to ensure accuracy and relevance.

Benefits of Effective Knowledge Management:

1. **Enhanced Service Quality**: Access to knowledge enables better decision-making, leading to improved service quality.

2. **Efficient Problem Resolution**: Knowledge-driven problem resolution reduces incident response and resolution times.

3. **Improved Efficiency**: Efficient knowledge retrieval and use streamline operations and service delivery.

4. **Innovation and Continuous Improvement**: A culture of knowledge sharing fosters innovation and supports continual service improvement.

5. **Reduced Training Time**: New employees can quickly access knowledge resources, reducing the time required for training and onboarding.

6. **Risk Mitigation**: Knowledge helps identify and mitigate risks and vulnerabilities in service delivery.

In conclusion, Knowledge Management is a foundational

practice within ITIL that nurtures the wellspring of wisdom within an organization. By systematically capturing, storing, sharing, and leveraging knowledge and information, organizations can enhance service quality, improve efficiency, foster innovation, and drive continuous improvement. Knowledge becomes a valuable asset that empowers the organization to adapt, thrive, and deliver exceptional IT services.

E. Transition Planning and Support in ITIL: Paving the Road to Change

Transition Planning and Support is a crucial process within the ITIL (Information Technology Infrastructure Library) framework, primarily situated in the Service Transition phase. This process ensures that the introduction of new or modified IT services into the live environment is carefully planned, coordinated, and supported. Transition Planning and Support play a pivotal role in minimizing risks, ensuring a smooth transition, and delivering value to customers and the business. In this comprehensive exploration, we'll delve into the world of Transition Planning and Support to understand its significance, objectives, processes, and benefits.

What Is Transition Planning and Support in ITIL?

Transition Planning and Support is the practice of planning and coordinating the transition of new or modified IT services into the live environment. This process encompasses activities related to planning, coordination, communication, and support to ensure that the changes are introduced effectively, with minimal disruption. The primary goal of Transition Planning and Support is to enable a seamless transition of IT services while aligning with business objectives and customer needs.

Key Objectives of Transition Planning and Support:

1. **Effective Planning**:

   - **Objective**: To plan and schedule the transition of changes, ensuring that they align with business requirements and objectives.

   - **Significance**: Effective planning minimizes risks and ensures that changes are introduced with precision.

2. **Coordination and Communication**:

   - **Objective**: To coordinate activities among various stakeholders and facilitate clear communication during the transition.

   - **Significance**: Coordination and communication are essential for ensuring a smooth transition and minimizing disruptions.

3. **Risk Management**:

- **Objective**: To identify and mitigate risks associated with the transition, ensuring that the live environment remains stable.

- **Significance**: Risk mitigation reduces the likelihood of service disruptions and unexpected consequences.

4. **Knowledge Transfer**:

- **Objective**: To transfer knowledge and information about the changes to the appropriate teams and individuals.

- **Significance**: Knowledge transfer ensures that everyone involved understands the changes and their impact.

Processes in Transition Planning and Support:

1. **Transition Planning**:

- **Process**: Involves planning and scheduling the transition of changes, including defining roles and responsibilities.

2. **Change Evaluation**:

- **Process**: Assesses the potential impact and risks of

proposed changes, determining whether they should proceed to the next stage.

3. **Change Approval**:

   - **Process**: Involves gaining approval from the Change Advisory Board (CAB) or relevant stakeholders to authorize the change's implementation.

4. **Release Deployment**:

   - **Process**: Coordinates the deployment of changes into the live environment, following carefully defined procedures and minimizing disruption.

5. **Early Life Support**:

   - **Process**: Provides support and assistance immediately after the deployment to address any issues that may arise.

6. **Knowledge Transfer**:

   - **Process**: Ensures that knowledge and information related to the transition are documented and accessible for future reference.

Benefits of Effective Transition Planning and Support:

1. **Minimized Disruption**: Effective planning and coordination

minimize the risk of service disruptions during the transition.

2. **Efficient Transition**: Changes are introduced efficiently, reducing the likelihood of errors and defects.

3. **Risk Reduction**: Identifying and mitigating risks associated with the transition reduces the impact of issues during deployment.

4. **Knowledge Sharing**: Knowledge transfer ensures that information related to the transition is documented and accessible for future reference.

5. **Alignment with Business Goals**: The transition aligns changes with business objectives, delivering value to the organization and customers.

In conclusion, Transition Planning and Support is a critical practice within ITIL that ensures changes are introduced into the live environment with precision, minimal disruption, and a relentless focus on delivering value to customers and the business. By adhering to the principles and processes of Transition Planning and Support, organizations can navigate the road to change with confidence, embracing transitions as opportunities for growth and improvement while maintaining the stability and continuity of IT services.

F. Change Evaluation in ITIL: Measuring the Impact of Transformation

Change Evaluation is a pivotal process within the ITIL (Information Technology Infrastructure Library) framework, primarily situated in the Service Transition phase. This process is responsible for assessing the potential impact and risks of proposed changes before they are implemented in the live environment. Change Evaluation plays a crucial role in ensuring that changes are introduced with precision and a clear understanding of their consequences. In this comprehensive exploration, we'll delve into the world of Change Evaluation to understand its significance, objectives, processes, and benefits.

What Is Change Evaluation in ITIL?

Change Evaluation is the practice of systematically assessing proposed changes to IT services and infrastructure before they are implemented. It aims to provide decision-makers with the necessary information to make informed choices about whether to proceed with a change or not. The primary goal of Change Evaluation is to minimize risks, ensure that changes align with business objectives, and prevent unnecessary disruptions.

Key Objectives of Change Evaluation:

1. **Risk Assessment**:

   - **Objective**: To assess the potential risks and impact of proposed changes on IT services and the organization.

- **Significance**: Risk assessment helps decision-makers make informed choices about whether to approve or reject changes.

2. **Change Prioritization**:

- **Objective**: To prioritize changes based on their impact, urgency, and business value.

- **Significance**: Prioritization ensures that critical changes are addressed promptly and that resources are allocated appropriately.

3. **Decision Support**:

- **Objective**: To provide decision-makers with the information needed to approve or reject proposed changes.

- **Significance**: Informed decisions lead to the implementation of changes that align with business goals and minimize disruptions.

Processes in Change Evaluation:

1. **Change Proposal Assessment**:

- **Process**: Involves assessing change proposals to

determine their potential impact, risks, and benefits.

2. **Change Impact Assessment**:

   - **Process**: Assesses the impact of proposed changes on IT services, infrastructure, and other areas.

3. **Risk Assessment**:

   - **Process**: Identifies and assesses risks associated with proposed changes and develops mitigation plans.

4. **Change Prioritization**:

   - **Process**: Prioritizes changes based on their impact, urgency, and business value.

5. **Decision Support**:

   - **Process**: Provides decision-makers with the necessary information to approve or reject proposed changes.

Benefits of Effective Change Evaluation:

1. **Risk Mitigation**: Change Evaluation identifies and assesses risks associated with changes, enabling organizations to develop mitigation plans.

2. **Effective Resource Allocation**: Prioritization ensures that resources are allocated to address the most critical changes first.

3. **Informed Decision-Making**: Decision support provides decision-makers with the information needed to make informed choices about changes.

4. **Minimized Disruption**: Assessing changes before implementation reduces the likelihood of service disruptions.

5. **Alignment with Business Goals**: Change Evaluation ensures that changes align with business objectives, delivering value to the organization and customers.

6. **Optimized Change Management**: Effective evaluation streamlines the Change Management process, making it more efficient and effective.

In conclusion, Change Evaluation is a critical practice within ITIL that ensures changes are assessed and understood before implementation. By systematically evaluating the potential impact and risks of changes, organizations can make informed decisions that align with business objectives and minimize disruptions. Change Evaluation empowers organizations to embrace change as an opportunity for growth and improvement while safeguarding the stability and continuity of IT services.

CHAPTER 6

ITIL Service Operation

ITIL Service Operation is a core component of the ITIL (Information Technology Infrastructure Library) framework, embodying the ongoing daily activities and practices that enable the delivery of IT services to customers and end-users. This phase is where IT services come to life, functioning as the beating heart that ensures the continual availability, performance, and support of services. In this introductory exploration, we embark on a journey into the realm of ITIL Service Operation to grasp its significance, objectives, and the pivotal role it plays in sustaining IT services.

Within ITIL Service Operation, IT professionals work diligently to maintain service quality, resolve incidents and problems, fulfill service requests, and monitor the health of IT services. This phase thrives on efficiency, effectiveness, and customer-centricity, all of which are essential to meet the ever-evolving needs of the organization and its users.

Join us as we venture deeper into ITIL Service Operation, where the magic of IT services happens, and where the relentless pursuit of service excellence ensures that IT supports the business

Mastering IT Service Management and Infrastructure Library
with precision, reliability, and a focus on delivering value.

A. Service Operation Principles in ITIL: Nurturing the Heart of IT Services

Service Operation in ITIL is the heartbeat of IT services, where the day-to-day activities and processes ensure the continual availability and performance of services. To maintain this rhythm, Service Operation relies on a set of principles that guide its activities and underpin the delivery of high-quality IT services. In this comprehensive exploration, we'll delve into these critical Service Operation principles to understand their significance and how they shape the operation of IT services.

1. Focus on Value to the Business:

- **Principle**: The primary focus of Service Operation is to deliver value to the business and its customers.

- **Significance**: This principle ensures that all activities and decisions are aligned with business objectives, emphasizing the importance of IT as a business enabler.

2. Organizational Structure:

- **Principle**: Service Operation should have a clear organizational structure with well-defined roles and responsibilities.

- **Significance**: An organized structure ensures that tasks are efficiently carried out, and accountability is established.

3. Built-In Resilience:

- **Principle**: IT services and infrastructure should be designed with built-in resilience to minimize the impact of failures.

- **Significance**: This principle aims to maintain service availability, even in the face of disruptions or incidents.

4. Standardization and Consistency:

- **Principle**: Standardization and consistency in processes and procedures help maintain service quality.

- **Significance**: Standardized processes reduce the likelihood of errors and make it easier to manage and support services.

5. Collaboration and Coordination:

- **Principle**: Collaboration and coordination among teams and departments are essential for effective Service Operation.

- **Significance**: Cooperation ensures that service delivery is seamless and that issues are resolved efficiently.

6. Automation and Technology:

- **Principle**: Leveraging automation and appropriate technology can enhance efficiency and reduce manual effort.

- **Significance**: Automation streamlines tasks, minimizes human error, and accelerates incident resolution.

7. Monitoring and Measurement:

- **Principle**: Monitoring and measurement of IT services and infrastructure are vital for proactive problem detection and performance improvement.

- **Significance**: This principle helps ensure that services meet agreed-upon performance standards.

8. Incident Management and Resolution:

- **Principle**: Rapid incident management and resolution are key to minimizing service disruptions and customer impact.

- **Significance**: Efficient incident management maintains service availability and customer satisfaction.

9. Continuous Improvement:

- **Principle**: Service Operation should embrace a culture of continuous improvement to enhance service quality and efficiency.

- **Significance**: Continuous improvement ensures that services evolve to meet changing business needs.

10. Customer-Centric Approach:

- **Principle**: A customer-centric approach means that Service Operation focuses on delivering value to customers and end-users.

- **Significance**: Customer satisfaction is paramount, and services should meet their needs and expectations.

In conclusion, Service Operation principles in ITIL provide the foundation for the efficient and effective delivery of IT services. By adhering to these principles, organizations can nurture the heart of IT services, ensuring their ongoing availability, performance, and support while continually delivering value to the business and its customers.

B. Incident Management in ITIL: Restoring Service Harmony

Incident Management is a fundamental process within the ITIL (Information Technology Infrastructure Library) framework, situated in the Service Operation phase. This process is the guardian of service harmony, responsible for restoring normal service operations as swiftly as possible when incidents disrupt the smooth flow of IT services. Incident Management is critical for minimizing the impact of incidents on business operations and customer satisfaction. In this comprehensive exploration, we'll delve into the world of Incident Management to understand its significance, objectives, processes, and benefits.

What Is Incident Management in ITIL?

Incident Management is the practice of efficiently and effectively managing incidents to minimize their impact on IT services and the organization. Incidents can range from minor service disruptions to major outages, and the goal of this process is to restore normal service operations as quickly as possible. Incident Management also includes the logging, categorization, prioritization, and resolution of incidents, ensuring that service disruptions are addressed with precision.

Key Objectives of Incident Management:

1. **Rapid Restoration**:

   - **Objective**: To restore normal service operations as swiftly as possible after an incident occurs.

   - **Significance**: Rapid restoration minimizes the impact of incidents on business operations and customer satisfaction.

2. **Effective Incident Logging**:

   - **Objective**: To log incidents accurately and comprehensively, capturing all relevant information.

- **Significance**: Effective incident logging ensures that incidents are properly documented for analysis and resolution.

3. **Categorization and Prioritization**:

   - **Objective**: To categorize and prioritize incidents based on their impact and urgency.

   - **Significance**: Categorization and prioritization help ensure that critical incidents receive immediate attention.

4. **Resolution and Recovery**:

   - **Objective**: To resolve incidents and restore services to their normal state.

   - **Significance**: Efficient resolution minimizes downtime and service disruptions.

Processes in Incident Management:

1. **Incident Identification and Logging**:

   - **Process**: Involves identifying incidents, logging them with detailed information, and assigning unique reference numbers.

2. **Incident Categorization and Prioritization**:

   - **Process**: Categorizes incidents based on predefined criteria and assigns priority levels.

3. **Incident Investigation and Diagnosis**:

   - **Process**: Investigates the root cause of incidents and determines the best course of action for resolution.

4. **Incident Resolution and Recovery**:

   - **Process**: Implements actions to resolve incidents, restore services, and verify that normal operations are resumed.

5. **Incident Closure**:

   - **Process**: Ensures that incidents are formally closed, documented, and communicated to relevant stakeholders.

Benefits of Effective Incident Management:

1. **Minimized Downtime**: Rapid incident resolution minimizes service downtime and disruption.

2. **Customer Satisfaction**: Efficient incident management enhances customer satisfaction by ensuring that services are available when needed.

3. **Resource Efficiency**: Resources are efficiently allocated to address and resolve incidents.

4. **Data for Improvement**: Incident data can be used for identifying recurring issues and improving service quality.

5. **Compliance and Reporting**: Effective incident management supports compliance requirements and enables accurate reporting.

In conclusion, Incident Management is a critical practice within ITIL that ensures IT services are restored to normal operations quickly and efficiently following incidents. By adhering to the principles and processes of Incident Management, organizations can minimize the impact of incidents on their business, maintain customer satisfaction, and ensure the smooth delivery of IT services.

C. Problem Management in ITIL: Eliminating the Root Causes of IT Issues

Problem Management is a pivotal process within the ITIL (Information Technology Infrastructure Library) framework, primarily situated in the Service Operation phase. This process is the detective of IT operations, focused on identifying and eliminating the root causes of incidents and problems to prevent recurring issues. Problem Management plays a crucial role in improving service quality, reducing incident frequency, and enhancing the overall stability of IT services. In this comprehensive exploration, we'll delve into the world of Problem Management to understand its significance, objectives, processes, and benefits.

What Is Problem Management in ITIL?

Problem Management is the practice of identifying and addressing the underlying causes of incidents and problems within IT services and infrastructure. While Incident Management focuses on restoring services quickly, Problem Management seeks to prevent incidents from occurring or recurring by addressing their root causes. This process involves investigation, analysis, and the development of permanent solutions to known issues.

Key Objectives of Problem Management:

1. **Root Cause Identification**:

   - **Objective**: To identify the underlying root causes of incidents and problems.

   - **Significance**: Identifying root causes is essential to prevent incidents from recurring.

2. **Incident Prevention**:

   - **Objective**: To develop and implement solutions that

prevent incidents from occurring.

- **Significance**: Preventing incidents enhances service quality and reduces disruption.

3. **Knowledge Management**:

- **Objective**: To ensure that knowledge about known problems and their solutions is documented and accessible.

- **Significance**: Knowledge sharing facilitates efficient problem resolution.

Processes in Problem Management:

1. **Problem Identification and Logging**:

- **Process**: Involves identifying and logging problems based on incident data and user reports.

2. **Problem Categorization and Prioritization**:

- **Process**: Categorizes and prioritizes problems based on their impact and urgency.

3. **Problem Investigation and Diagnosis**:

- **Process**: Investigates the root cause of problems, often involving technical analysis and collaboration with subject matter experts.

4. **Permanent Solution Development**:

   - **Process**: Develops and tests permanent solutions to address the root causes of problems.

5. **Problem Closure**:

   - **Process**: Ensures that problems are formally closed, documented, and communicated to relevant stakeholders.

Benefits of Effective Problem Management:

1. **Incident Prevention**: Effective Problem Management prevents incidents from occurring or recurring, reducing service disruption.

2. **Enhanced Service Quality**: By addressing root causes, service quality is improved, leading to higher customer satisfaction.

3. **Resource Efficiency**: Resources are efficiently allocated to address and eliminate the root causes of problems.

4. **Knowledge Sharing**: Knowledge management ensures that information about known problems and solutions is accessible for future reference.

5. **Continuous Improvement**: Problem Management supports a culture of continuous improvement by addressing recurring

issues and driving service enhancements.

In conclusion, Problem Management is a critical practice within ITIL that focuses on eliminating the root causes of incidents and problems to prevent recurrence. By adhering to the principles and processes of Problem Management, organizations can improve service quality, reduce service disruptions, and enhance the overall stability and reliability of IT services.

D. Request Fulfillment in ITIL: Meeting the Demands of Service Users

Request Fulfillment is an essential process within the ITIL (Information Technology Infrastructure Library) framework, primarily situated in the Service Operation phase. This process is the facilitator of service user needs and requests, ensuring that service users' demands for information, services, or resources are met efficiently and effectively. Request Fulfillment plays a critical role in enhancing customer satisfaction, streamlining service delivery, and optimizing resource allocation. In this comprehensive exploration, we'll delve into the world of Request Fulfillment to understand its significance, objectives, processes, and benefits.

What Is Request Fulfillment in ITIL?

Request Fulfillment is the practice of efficiently managing and processing service requests from service users and customers. These requests can vary widely, encompassing anything from access rights and hardware provisioning to software installations and information inquiries. The primary goal of Request Fulfillment is to ensure that service user requests are addressed promptly, following defined procedures and service level agreements (SLAs).

Key Objectives of Request Fulfillment:

1. **Efficient Request Handling**:

   - **Objective**: To handle service requests efficiently, ensuring that they are addressed within agreed-upon timeframes.

   - **Significance**: Efficient handling minimizes delays and enhances service user satisfaction.

2. **Standardized Processes**:

   - **Objective**: To establish standardized procedures for handling common types of service requests.

   - **Significance**: Standardization reduces errors and streamlines request processing.

3. **Compliance and Control**:

   - **Objective**: To ensure that requests are handled in

compliance with organizational policies and regulations.

- **Significance**: Compliance safeguards data security and legal requirements.

Processes in Request Fulfillment:

1. **Request Logging and Triage**:

   - **Process**: Involves logging incoming service requests, categorizing them, and determining their priority.

2. **Request Fulfillment**:

   - **Process**: Focuses on processing and fulfilling service requests, following standardized procedures and service level agreements (SLAs).

3. **Request Closure and Documentation**:

   - **Process**: Ensures that requests are formally closed, documented, and communicated to relevant stakeholders.

Benefits of Effective Request Fulfillment:

1. **Enhanced Customer Satisfaction**: Efficient request handling and prompt fulfillment lead to higher customer satisfaction.

2. **Streamlined Service Delivery**: Standardized processes

reduce request processing times and improve resource allocation.

3. **Resource Optimization**: Resources are allocated efficiently, ensuring that requests are addressed without unnecessary delays.

4. **Compliance and Control**: Request Fulfillment processes ensure that requests are handled in compliance with policies and regulations.

5. **Knowledge Sharing**: Knowledge management ensures that information related to request fulfillment is documented and accessible.

In conclusion, Request Fulfillment is a critical practice within ITIL that ensures service user requests are addressed promptly, efficiently, and in compliance with organizational policies and SLAs. By adhering to the principles and processes of Request Fulfillment, organizations can enhance customer satisfaction, streamline service delivery, optimize resource allocation, and meet the diverse demands of service users effectively.

E. Event Management in ITIL: Navigating the Digital Landscape with Precision

Event Management is a crucial process within the ITIL (Information Technology Infrastructure Library) framework, primarily situated in the Service Operation phase. This process is the sentinel of the IT environment, responsible for monitoring, detecting, and responding to events that occur within the IT infrastructure. Event Management plays a pivotal role in maintaining service availability, identifying potential issues, and proactively addressing them before they escalate into incidents. In this comprehensive exploration, we'll delve into the world of Event Management to understand its significance, objectives, processes, and benefits.

What Is Event Management in ITIL?

Event Management is the practice of systematically monitoring and responding to events that occur within the IT environment. Events can encompass a wide range of activities, from hardware failures and system errors to security breaches and performance fluctuations. The primary goal of Event Management is to identify and respond to events promptly, ensuring that potential issues are detected and addressed before they impact service availability.

Key Objectives of Event Management:

1. **Proactive Monitoring**:

   - **Objective**: To proactively monitor the IT environment for events that may indicate potential issues or deviations from normal operations.

- **Significance**: Proactive monitoring allows for early detection and response, minimizing service disruptions.

2. **Event Correlation**:

   - **Objective**: To correlate and analyze events to identify patterns or trends that may require further investigation.

   - **Significance**: Event correlation helps uncover underlying issues and dependencies within the IT infrastructure.

3. **Automated Response**:

   - **Objective**: To automate responses to predefined events, enabling rapid mitigation of known issues.

   - **Significance**: Automated responses reduce manual intervention and accelerate incident resolution.

Processes in Event Management:

1. **Event Detection and Monitoring**:

   - **Process**: Involves the continuous monitoring of the IT environment for events and activities that may indicate potential issues.

2. **Event Filtering and Categorization**:

    - **Process**: Filters and categorizes events based on predefined criteria, allowing for efficient handling and prioritization.

3. **Event Correlation and Analysis**:

    - **Process**: Correlates and analyzes events to identify patterns, trends, or anomalies that may require further investigation.

4. **Automated Response**:

    - **Process**: Implements predefined automated responses to specific events, such as restarting services or escalating incidents.

5. **Manual Intervention**:

    - **Process**: Involves manual intervention when events require human judgment and decision-making.

6. **Event Closure and Documentation**:

    - **Process**: Ensures that events are formally closed, documented, and communicated to relevant stakeholders.

Benefits of Effective Event Management:

1. **Proactive Issue Resolution**: Early event detection and response prevent potential issues from escalating into incidents.

2. **Improved Service Availability**: Timely event management minimizes service downtime and disruptions.

3. **Efficient Resource Allocation**: Resources are allocated efficiently to address events based on their impact and urgency.

4. **Automation**: Automated responses reduce manual intervention, saving time and resources.

5. **Enhanced Security**: Event management helps detect and respond to security breaches and anomalies.

In conclusion, Event Management is a critical practice within ITIL that ensures the proactive monitoring and response to events within the IT environment. By adhering to the principles and processes of Event Management, organizations can maintain service availability, identify potential issues, and navigate the digital landscape with precision and confidence. Event Management stands as a vigilant guardian, ready to respond to the subtle signals that may foretell potential IT disruptions.

F. Access Management in ITIL: Safeguarding Digital Frontiers with Precision

Access Management is a vital process within the ITIL (Information Technology Infrastructure Library) framework, primarily situated in the Service Operation phase. This process serves as the guardian of digital frontiers, responsible for ensuring that individuals and entities have the appropriate access rights to IT services and systems. Access Management plays a pivotal role in safeguarding information security, protecting data integrity, and preventing unauthorized access to critical resources. In this comprehensive exploration, we'll delve into the world of Access Management to understand its significance, objectives, processes, and benefits.

What Is Access Management in ITIL?

Access Management is the practice of granting, modifying, monitoring, and revoking access to IT services, systems, and data based on predefined policies and procedures. It encompasses a range of activities, from user provisioning and authentication to access control and permissions management. The primary goal of Access Management is to ensure that only authorized individuals or entities can access and use IT resources while protecting against unauthorized access and security breaches.

Key Objectives of Access Management:

1. **Access Control**:

   - **Objective**: To control and manage user access to IT services and data based on their roles and responsibilities.

   - **Significance**: Access control ensures that individuals have the appropriate level of access to perform their job functions.

2. **User Authentication**:

   - **Objective**: To verify the identity of users and entities seeking access through authentication and authorization.

   - **Significance**: User authentication ensures that only authorized individuals can access resources.

3. **Access Provisioning and De-provisioning**:

   - **Objective**: To efficiently provision and de-provision user access as individuals join, change roles, or leave the organization.

   - **Significance**: Proper access provisioning and de-provisioning reduce the risk of unauthorized access.

Processes in Access Management:

1. **Access Request Management**:

   - **Process**: Involves handling and fulfilling access requests from users, including new access requests, modifications, and revocations.

2. **User Authentication and Authorization**:

   - **Process**: Validates user identities, verifies access rights, and enforces access control policies.

3. **Access Monitoring and Review**:

   - **Process**: Monitors user access activities, reviews access rights, and conducts periodic access audits.

4. **Access Revocation**:

   - **Process**: Revokes access rights when users no longer require access or when security concerns arise.

Benefits of Effective Access Management:

1. **Enhanced Information Security**: Access Management safeguards against unauthorized access, reducing the risk of data breaches.

2. **Data Integrity**: Access control ensures that data is accessed and modified only by authorized personnel.

3. **Compliance**: Proper access management supports compliance with regulatory requirements and security standards.

4. **Efficient Resource Allocation**: Resources are efficiently allocated based on access needs, reducing waste and improving resource utilization.

5. **User Productivity**: Users have the appropriate access to perform their job functions without unnecessary delays.

In conclusion, Access Management is a critical practice within ITIL that ensures the appropriate access rights to IT services and resources while safeguarding information security and data integrity. By adhering to the principles and processes of Access Management, organizations can protect against unauthorized access, maintain compliance, and safeguard the digital frontiers of their IT environment with precision and confidence. Access Management stands as a vigilant guardian, allowing authorized users to access resources while keeping unauthorized access at bay.

CHAPTER 7

ITIL Continual Service Improvement (CSI)

ITIL Continual Service Improvement (CSI) is not just a phase but a perpetual journey of excellence within the ITIL (Information Technology Infrastructure Library) framework. It is a dynamic and ongoing process that focuses on enhancing IT services, processes, and overall performance. CSI emphasizes the never-ending quest for improvement, encouraging organizations to continually assess, analyze, and refine their services and operations. In this introductory exploration, we embark on a journey into the realm of ITIL CSI to understand its significance, objectives, and the transformative role it plays in elevating service delivery.

Within ITIL CSI, the goal is not merely to meet current standards but to surpass them consistently. This phase thrives on data-driven decision-making, iterative improvements, and a culture of innovation. By continually striving for betterment, organizations can adapt to changing business needs, enhance customer satisfaction, and remain competitive in the dynamic world of IT services.

Join us as we venture deeper into ITIL CSI, where the pursuit of excellence knows no bounds, and the commitment to continuous improvement fuels the evolution of IT services towards perfection.

A. CSI Principles and Concepts in ITIL: The Pillars of Continuous Improvement

Continual Service Improvement (CSI) in ITIL (Information Technology Infrastructure Library) is not just a process; it's a mindset, a philosophy, and a set of principles and concepts that drive organizations to relentlessly pursue excellence in their IT services. At its core, CSI seeks to improve the efficiency, effectiveness, and quality of IT services and processes through a systematic and iterative approach. In this comprehensive exploration, we'll delve into the fundamental CSI principles and concepts that underpin the journey of continuous improvement.

1. Focus on Improvement:

- **Principle**: CSI is centered around the idea that there's always room for improvement.

- **Significance**: The relentless pursuit of improvement ensures that services evolve to meet changing business needs and customer expectations.

2. The Deming Cycle (PDCA):

- **Concept**: The Plan-Do-Check-Act (PDCA) cycle is a cornerstone of CSI, representing a systematic approach to continuous improvement.

- **Significance**: PDCA provides a structured framework for identifying areas for improvement, implementing changes, monitoring results, and adjusting strategies as needed.

3. CSI Register:

- **Concept**: The CSI Register is a repository for recording improvement opportunities, ideas, and initiatives.

- **Significance**: It helps organizations systematically track and prioritize improvement initiatives, ensuring that they are addressed in an organized manner.

4. Key Performance Indicators (KPIs):

- **Concept**: KPIs are used to measure the performance and effectiveness of IT services and processes.

- **Significance**: By tracking KPIs, organizations gain insights into areas that require improvement and can make data-driven decisions.

5. Service Level Management (SLM):

- **Concept**: SLM is closely tied to CSI, as it involves defining, monitoring, and improving service levels.

- **Significance**: SLM ensures that services align with business needs and customer expectations, and it provides a foundation for continuous service improvement.

**6. The 7-Step Improvement Process:

- **Concept**: This process provides a structured approach for identifying improvement opportunities, defining measurable objectives, and implementing and sustaining improvements.

- **Significance**: The 7-step process guides organizations through the CSI journey, from recognizing the need for improvement to realizing measurable benefits.

**7. Data-Driven Decision-Making:

- **Principle**: CSI relies on data and evidence to drive decision-making.

- **Significance**: Data analysis helps organizations identify trends, root causes of issues, and areas for improvement, ensuring that changes are made based on facts, not assumptions.

8. **Continual Feedback Loop**:

- **Principle**: CSI promotes a culture of open communication and feedback.

- **Significance**: Feedback from stakeholders, users, and teams is invaluable in identifying improvement opportunities and ensuring that services meet expectations.

9. **Measuring Success**:

- **Principle**: Success in CSI is measured by the achievement of predefined objectives and the realization of tangible benefits.

- **Significance**: Setting clear objectives and measuring success ensures that improvements deliver real value to the organization.

In conclusion, CSI principles and concepts form the foundation of the continual improvement journey in ITIL. By embracing these principles and applying these concepts, organizations can create a culture of continuous improvement, enhance service quality, and adapt to the ever-evolving landscape of IT services and technology. CSI is not a destination but a never-ending expedition towards service excellence and customer satisfaction.

B. The CSI Approach in ITIL: A Systematic Path to Continuous Improvement

The CSI (Continual Service Improvement) approach in ITIL (Information Technology Infrastructure Library) is a structured and systematic method for achieving and sustaining continuous improvement in IT services and processes. Unlike a one-time project, the CSI approach is an ongoing journey that emphasizes the need for regular assessment, analysis, and refinement of IT services. It provides organizations with the means to evolve and adapt to changing business needs and technological advancements. In this comprehensive exploration, we'll delve into the CSI approach to understand its significance, objectives, phases, and benefits.

What Is the CSI Approach in ITIL?

The CSI approach in ITIL is a methodical and iterative framework that guides organizations in identifying opportunities for improvement, defining objectives, implementing changes, and monitoring progress. It is based on the PDCA (Plan-Do-Check-Act) cycle, a concept popularized by W. Edwards Deming, and it's designed to ensure that improvements are made in a controlled and sustainable manner.

Key Objectives of the CSI Approach:

1. **Continuous Improvement**:

   - **Objective**: To instill a culture of continual improvement within the organization.

   - **Significance**: Continual improvement ensures that IT services evolve to meet changing business needs and customer expectations.

2. **Data-Driven Decision-Making**:

   - **Objective**: To make informed decisions based on data, evidence, and analysis.

   - **Significance**: Data-driven decisions lead to more effective improvements and prevent changes based on assumptions.

3. **Alignment with Business Objectives**:

   - **Objective**: To ensure that improvements align with the strategic goals and objectives of the organization.

   - **Significance**: Alignment with business objectives ensures that improvements are relevant and contribute to organizational success.

Phases of the CSI Approach:

1. **Identify the Strategy for Improvement**:

    - **Phase**: This phase involves identifying areas and opportunities for improvement, often based on data, performance metrics, and feedback.

2. **Define What Will Be Measured**:

    - **Phase**: Organizations must define key performance indicators (KPIs) and metrics that will be used to measure the success of improvement efforts.

3. **Gather the Data**:

    - **Phase**: Data is collected, often through surveys, monitoring tools, and analysis of existing performance data.

4. **Process the Data**:

    - **Phase**: Data is analyzed to identify trends, patterns, and areas that require attention.

5. **Analyze the Information and Data**:

    - **Phase**: Information and data are used to identify areas for improvement and set specific, measurable objectives.

6. **Present and Use the Information**:

- **Phase**: Findings and improvement recommendations are presented to stakeholders, and decisions are made regarding which improvements to pursue.

7. **Implement Improvement**:

- **Phase**: Improvement initiatives are planned, executed, and monitored, with a focus on achieving the defined objectives.

8. **Review and Analyze**:

- **Phase**: The results of improvement initiatives are reviewed and analyzed to determine if objectives have been met.

9. **Apply Lessons Learned**:

- **Phase**: Lessons learned from the improvement process are documented and applied to future improvement efforts.

Benefits of the CSI Approach:

1. **Continuous Service Improvement**: The CSI approach ensures that services and processes are continually refined to meet evolving needs.

2. **Data-Driven Decision-Making**: Organizations make informed decisions based on evidence and analysis.

3. **Alignment with Business Objectives**: Improvement efforts are directly tied to organizational goals, ensuring relevance and value.

4. **Increased Efficiency and Effectiveness**: CSI leads to more efficient and effective IT services and processes.

5. **Enhanced Customer Satisfaction**: Continual improvement results in services that better meet customer expectations.

In conclusion, the CSI approach in ITIL is a systematic and structured framework for achieving and sustaining continuous improvement in IT services and processes. By following the phases of the CSI approach and embracing a culture of continual improvement, organizations can adapt to changing business needs, enhance service quality, and remain competitive in the ever-evolving landscape of IT services. The CSI approach is not just a methodology; it's a commitment to excellence and a blueprint for ongoing success.

C. Key Metrics and Measurements in ITIL CSI: Navigating Improvement with Data

In ITIL (Information Technology Infrastructure Library) CSI (Continual Service Improvement), metrics and measurements play a pivotal role in the journey toward excellence. They provide organizations with valuable insights into the performance of IT services, processes, and improvements. Metrics and measurements are not just numbers; they are the compass that guides organizations toward informed decision-making and continuous improvement. In this comprehensive exploration, we'll delve into the significance, objectives, types, and application of key metrics and measurements in ITIL CSI.

Significance of Key Metrics and Measurements in CSI:

1. **Informed Decision-Making**:

   - **Significance**: Metrics and measurements provide data-driven insights, enabling informed decision-making at all levels of the organization.

2. **Continuous Improvement**:

   - **Significance**: Metrics help identify areas for improvement, track progress, and measure the success of improvement initiatives.

3. **Service Quality and Performance**:

   - **Significance**: Metrics gauge the quality and performance of IT services, ensuring they meet customer expectations.

4. **Resource Optimization**:

  - **Significance**: Metrics help optimize resource allocation, reducing waste and improving efficiency.

5. **Customer Satisfaction**:

  - **Significance**: Metrics related to service quality and customer feedback contribute to enhanced customer satisfaction.

Objectives of Key Metrics and Measurements in CSI:

1. **Identify Improvement Opportunities**:

  - **Objective**: To identify areas where improvements are needed based on performance data.

2. **Measure Progress**:

  - **Objective**: To track the progress of improvement initiatives and ensure they are on target.

3. **Verify Achievements**:

  - **Objective**: To measure the success of improvement efforts against predefined objectives.

4. **Support Informed Decision-Making**:

  - **Objective**: To provide data that supports data-driven

decision-making regarding improvements and investments.

5. **Align with Business Goals**:

- **Objective**: To ensure that metrics and measurements align with organizational objectives and customer needs.

Types of Key Metrics and Measurements in CSI:

1. **Performance Metrics**:

- **Type**: These metrics measure the performance of IT services and processes, such as response times, uptime, and availability.

2. **Customer Satisfaction Metrics**:

- **Type**: These metrics assess customer satisfaction and feedback, often gathered through surveys and feedback mechanisms.

3. **Efficiency Metrics**:

- **Type**: Efficiency metrics measure the efficiency of resource utilization, cost per transaction, and resource optimization.

4. **Quality Metrics**:

- **Type**: Quality metrics assess the quality of IT services, including error rates, defect density, and adherence to standards.

5. **Capacity and Resource Metrics**:

- **Type**: These metrics measure the capacity and resource utilization, helping organizations ensure they have the right resources in place.

6. **Service Level Agreement (SLA) Metrics**:

- **Type**: SLA metrics measure the performance of services against agreed-upon service level agreements.

Application of Key Metrics and Measurements in CSI:

1. **Baseline Establishment**:

- **Application**: Metrics establish a baseline for current performance, serving as a reference point for improvement initiatives.

2. **Continuous Monitoring**:

- **Application**: Metrics are continually monitored to track performance and identify deviations or trends that require attention.

3. **Problem Identification**:

- **Application**: Metrics help identify areas where issues or bottlenecks exist within services or processes.

4. **Progress Tracking**:

- **Application**: Metrics track the progress of improvement initiatives, ensuring they stay on course and meet predefined objectives.

5. **Performance Evaluation**:

- **Application**: Metrics evaluate the performance of IT services and processes against established standards and expectations.

6. **Feedback Integration**:

- **Application**: Customer feedback and satisfaction metrics inform improvement efforts and drive enhancements.

In conclusion, key metrics and measurements are the lifeblood of CSI in ITIL. They provide organizations with the data and insights needed to navigate the path of continuous improvement. By defining, collecting, analyzing, and applying metrics, organizations can make informed decisions, track progress, and ensure that IT services evolve to meet changing business needs and customer expectations. Metrics and measurements transform improvement from a vague aspiration into a concrete, data-driven journey towards excellence.

D. Implementing CSI in ITSM: A Blueprint for Service Excellence

Implementing CSI (Continual Service Improvement) within ITSM (IT Service Management) is a strategic endeavor that empowers organizations to evolve, adapt, and excel in delivering IT services. It's a commitment to an ongoing cycle of assessment, analysis, refinement, and innovation. By integrating CSI into ITSM, organizations ensure that their services continually align with business needs and customer expectations. In this comprehensive exploration, we'll delve into the significance, objectives, steps, and best practices for implementing CSI in ITSM.

Significance of Implementing CSI in ITSM:

1. **Service Evolution**:

   - **Significance**: Implementing CSI ensures that IT services evolve to meet changing business requirements and technological advancements.

2. **Customer-Centricity**:

   - **Significance**: CSI helps ITSM shift its focus towards customer needs, resulting in enhanced customer satisfaction.

3. **Efficiency and Effectiveness**:

   - **Significance**: CSI identifies opportunities for efficiency improvements, leading to more effective service delivery.

4. **Data-Driven Decision-Making**:

   - **Significance**: Implementing CSI promotes data-driven decision-making by providing insights into service performance.

Objectives of Implementing CSI in ITSM:

1. **Continuous Improvement Culture**:

   - **Objective**: To foster a culture of continual improvement within the organization.

2. **Service Alignment**:

   - **Objective**: To ensure that IT services align with business objectives and customer expectations.

3. **Efficiency Enhancement**:

- **Objective**: To identify and implement efficiency enhancements within ITSM processes and services.

4. **Data Utilization**:

- **Objective**: To leverage data and insights to make informed decisions and drive improvements.

5. **Customer Satisfaction**:

- **Objective**: To enhance customer satisfaction by delivering services that consistently meet or exceed expectations.

Steps for Implementing CSI in ITSM:

1. **Establish CSI Governance**:

- **Step**: Develop a governance framework that defines roles, responsibilities, and accountability for CSI initiatives.

2. **Define Clear Objectives**:

- **Step**: Set clear and measurable objectives for CSI efforts, ensuring alignment with organizational goals.

3. **Collect Data and Metrics**:

- **Step**: Implement data collection mechanisms and define key performance indicators (KPIs) to assess the current state of IT services.

4. **Analyze and Identify Improvements**:

- **Step**: Analyze collected data to identify areas for improvement and prioritize them based on business impact.

5. **Plan Improvement Initiatives**:

- **Step**: Develop detailed improvement plans, specifying goals, resources, timelines, and success criteria.

6. **Implement Improvements**:

- **Step**: Execute improvement initiatives, monitoring progress and making adjustments as necessary.

7. **Monitor and Measure**:

- **Step**: Continually monitor the impact of improvements by measuring KPIs and assessing results against objectives.

8. **Review and Learn**:

- **Step**: Conduct regular reviews of improvement

initiatives, capturing lessons learned and applying them to future efforts.

9. **Feedback Integration**:

- **Step**: Incorporate feedback from customers, stakeholders, and service users to drive further improvements.

10. **Document and Communicate**:

- **Step**: Maintain records of improvement initiatives and communicate their impact to relevant stakeholders.

Best Practices for Implementing CSI in ITSM:

1. **Engage Stakeholders**: Involve all relevant stakeholders, including customers and end-users, in the CSI process to gather diverse perspectives.

2. **Focus on Data Quality**: Ensure that data collected for analysis is accurate, relevant, and up-to-date.

3. **Iterative Approach**: Embrace an iterative approach to improvement, where each cycle builds on the insights and successes of the previous one.

4. **Measurement Alignment**: Ensure that KPIs and metrics align with both organizational goals and customer expectations.

5. **Cultural Change**: Promote a culture of continuous improvement throughout the organization, emphasizing collaboration and innovation.

6. **Knowledge Sharing**: Encourage knowledge sharing and documentation of best practices to facilitate ongoing learning.

In conclusion, implementing CSI in ITSM is not just a practice; it's a journey toward service excellence and customer satisfaction. By following a structured approach, setting clear objectives, and embracing a culture of continual improvement, organizations can enhance their IT services, optimize processes, and remain agile in an ever-changing digital landscape. CSI in ITSM is not a destination but a perpetual pursuit of excellence, ensuring that IT services consistently deliver value to the organization and its customers.

E. Fostering a Continuous Improvement Culture: The Heartbeat of Organizational Excellence

A continuous improvement culture is the lifeblood of organizations striving for excellence. It's not just a buzzword; it's a philosophy, a mindset, and a commitment to ongoing betterment. Such a culture promotes the idea that every individual and process can be enhanced, leading to improved outcomes, increased efficiency, and greater customer satisfaction. In this comprehensive exploration, we'll delve into the significance, principles, strategies, and benefits of fostering a continuous improvement culture within organizations.

Significance of a Continuous Improvement Culture:

1. **Enhanced Performance**:

    - **Significance**: A culture of continuous improvement drives organizations to consistently outperform themselves.

2. **Customer-Centricity**:

    - **Significance**: It places customers at the center, aligning products and services with their needs and preferences.

3. **Adaptability**:

    - **Significance**: A culture of continuous improvement prepares organizations to adapt to change, remain relevant, and thrive in dynamic environments.

4. **Employee Engagement**:

    - **Significance**: Engaged employees are more likely to contribute ideas and efforts toward improvement, leading to better outcomes.

5. **Innovation**:

- **Significance**: Continuous improvement often leads to innovation, helping organizations stay competitive and seize new opportunities.

Principles of a Continuous Improvement Culture:

1. **Embrace Change**:

- **Principle**: Embrace change as an opportunity for growth and development, not as a disruption.

2. **Data-Driven Decisions**:

- **Principle**: Base decisions on data, facts, and evidence rather than assumptions.

3. **Feedback Loops**:

- **Principle**: Establish feedback mechanisms to capture insights from employees, customers, and stakeholders.

4. **Ownership and Accountability**:

- **Principle**: Encourage individuals to take ownership of their work and be accountable for outcomes.

5. **Continuous Learning**:

- **Principle**: Cultivate a culture of learning and

development, where mistakes are viewed as opportunities to improve.

6. **Teamwork and Collaboration**:

- **Principle**: Promote teamwork and collaboration to generate diverse perspectives and ideas.

Strategies for Fostering a Continuous Improvement Culture:

1. **Leadership Commitment**:

- **Strategy**: Leadership should lead by example, demonstrating a commitment to continuous improvement and setting expectations for the entire organization.

2. **Clear Communication**:

- **Strategy**: Communicate the importance of continuous improvement, its benefits, and how individuals can contribute to it.

3. **Training and Development**:

- **Strategy**: Invest in training and development programs that equip employees with the skills and knowledge needed for improvement initiatives.

4. **Recognition and Rewards**:

- **Strategy**: Recognize and reward employees for their contributions to continuous improvement, fostering a culture of appreciation.

5. **Process Improvement Frameworks**:

- **Strategy**: Implement process improvement frameworks like Six Sigma, Lean, or ITIL to provide structured approaches to improvement.

6. **Innovation Initiatives**:

- **Strategy**: Encourage innovation initiatives that allow employees to explore new ideas and approaches.

Benefits of a Continuous Improvement Culture:

1. **Enhanced Efficiency and Productivity**:

- **Benefit**: Continuous improvement streamlines processes, reducing waste and boosting productivity.

2. **Customer Satisfaction**:

- **Benefit**: Improved products and services meet or exceed customer expectations, leading to higher satisfaction.

3. **Innovation and Adaptability**:

- **Benefit**: A culture of improvement fosters innovation and adaptability, helping organizations stay competitive.

4. **Employee Engagement**:

- **Benefit**: Engaged employees are more committed, motivated, and productive contributors to the organization's success.

5. **Better Problem-Solving**:

- **Benefit**: A culture of continuous improvement sharpens problem-solving skills, enabling quicker and more effective solutions.

In conclusion, fostering a continuous improvement culture is not just an organizational strategy; it's a commitment to perpetual betterment. Organizations that embrace this culture are better equipped to adapt to change, meet customer needs, and excel in their respective industries. A continuous improvement culture isn't a destination; it's the journey itself, where every day brings new opportunities to enhance, innovate, and excel. It's a mindset that propels organizations toward excellence, one step at a time.

CHAPTER 8

ITSM Beyond ITIL

While ITIL (Information Technology Infrastructure Library) has long been a cornerstone of IT Service Management (ITSM), the landscape of service management is constantly evolving. "ITSM Beyond ITIL" signifies a shift in focus, acknowledging that modern organizations need a more diverse and adaptable approach to meet the ever-changing demands of the digital age. In this introductory exploration, we venture into the realm of "ITSM Beyond ITIL" to understand its significance, emerging frameworks, and the evolving challenges and opportunities that await in the world of service management.

As technology continues to advance and organizations become increasingly interconnected, the traditional ITIL framework faces new challenges and complexities. ITSM must now extend its reach beyond IT operations to encompass broader business functions and align with emerging trends like Agile, DevOps, and Cloud Computing. "ITSM Beyond ITIL" represents a paradigm shift that recognizes the need for more comprehensive and agile service management approaches.

Join us as we embark on a journey to explore "ITSM Beyond

ITIL," where the boundaries of service management are expanding, and new frameworks and methodologies are emerging to meet the evolving needs of modern organizations.

A. Beyond ITIL: Exploring Other ITSM Frameworks

While ITIL (Information Technology Infrastructure Library) has been the gold standard in IT Service Management (ITSM) for decades, the ever-evolving landscape of technology and business demands has given rise to a variety of alternative ITSM frameworks and methodologies. These frameworks offer diverse approaches to managing IT services and are often tailored to specific organizational needs and goals. In this in-depth exploration, we'll delve into some of the most prominent ITSM frameworks beyond ITIL and their significance in modern service management.

1. COBIT (Control Objectives for Information and Related Technologies):

- **Significance**: COBIT is known for its focus on governance and aligning IT with business goals. It provides a comprehensive framework for managing and governing IT processes.

- **Key Features**: COBIT emphasizes control and compliance, making it valuable for organizations with stringent regulatory requirements.

2. ISO/IEC 20000:

- **Significance**: ISO/IEC 20000 is an international standard for IT service management, offering a structured framework for service delivery and quality management.

- **Key Features**: It focuses on aligning IT services with business needs and includes a certification process to demonstrate compliance.

3. Lean IT:

- **Significance**: Lean IT is inspired by lean manufacturing principles and aims to eliminate waste, streamline processes, and improve efficiency in IT operations.

- **Key Features**: It emphasizes continuous improvement, customer value, and the reduction of non-value-adding activities.

4. Agile and DevOps:

- **Significance**: Agile and DevOps are not traditional ITSM frameworks, but they are transforming IT service delivery by promoting collaboration, automation, and rapid deployment.

- **Key Features**: Agile emphasizes iterative development and

181

customer collaboration, while DevOps focuses on streamlining software delivery through automation and collaboration between development and IT operations.

5. SIAM (Service Integration and Management):

- **Significance**: SIAM is designed for organizations that rely on multiple service providers. It focuses on integrating and coordinating services from various providers to deliver a seamless experience to customers.

- **Key Features**: SIAM helps organizations manage complex service ecosystems and maintain control over service quality.

6. VeriSM:

- **Significance**: VeriSM is a more flexible and adaptive approach to ITSM, emphasizing value, outcomes, and collaboration across different management practices.

- **Key Features**: VeriSM recognizes that not all organizations have the same needs and encourages the integration of various management approaches to achieve business goals.

7. IT4IT:

- **Significance**: IT4IT, backed by The Open Group, focuses on managing the IT value chain from strategy to operations, providing a blueprint for how IT can deliver business value.

- **Key Features**: It defines a reference architecture and value streams for managing IT services efficiently.

8. ServiceNow ITSM:

- **Significance**: ServiceNow offers a comprehensive ITSM platform that combines ITIL principles with modern technology, enabling organizations to streamline service management processes.

- **Key Features**: ServiceNow ITSM includes a wide range of ITSM capabilities, including incident management, change management, and self-service portals.

9. FitSM:

- **Significance**: FitSM is a lightweight ITSM standard designed for smaller organizations or those looking for a more straightforward approach to service management.

- **Key Features**: It provides a simplified set of processes and guidelines for effective service management.

10. ITIL 4:

- **Significance**: ITIL 4, while building on the foundation of ITIL, introduces a more flexible and holistic approach to service management, accommodating modern practices like Agile and DevOps.

- **Key Features**: ITIL 4 includes the Service Value System (SVS) and emphasizes the co-creation of value with customers.

Choosing the Right Framework:

Selecting the most suitable ITSM framework or combination of frameworks depends on an organization's specific needs, industry, size, and existing processes. Many organizations even adopt a hybrid approach, combining elements from multiple frameworks to create a customized ITSM strategy that aligns with their unique circumstances.

In conclusion, the world of ITSM has expanded far beyond ITIL, offering organizations a rich tapestry of frameworks and methodologies to choose from. The key to success lies in understanding your organization's goals, challenges, and culture to select or adapt a framework that best supports your journey toward service excellence and customer satisfaction.

B. Integrating ITSM with Agile and DevOps: A Synergistic Approach to Service Excellence

The integration of IT Service Management (ITSM) with Agile and DevOps practices represents a transformative shift in the way organizations deliver IT services. Traditionally, ITSM, Agile, and DevOps were seen as separate disciplines, but their convergence offers the potential for enhanced service quality, faster delivery, and increased customer satisfaction. In this in-depth exploration, we'll delve into the significance, principles, strategies, and benefits of integrating ITSM with Agile and DevOps.

Significance of Integrating ITSM with Agile and DevOps:

1. **Speed and Responsiveness**:

   - **Significance**: Agile and DevOps emphasize rapid development and deployment, enabling ITSM to respond quickly to changing business needs and customer demands.

2. **Quality and Efficiency**:

   - **Significance**: Integrating ITSM with Agile and DevOps promotes a culture of continuous improvement, resulting in higher service quality and increased efficiency.

3. **Alignment with Business Goals**:

   - **Significance**: It aligns IT services with business objectives, ensuring that ITSM delivers value and supports strategic initiatives.

4. **Enhanced Collaboration**:

   - **Significance**: Collaboration between development,

operations, and ITSM teams leads to better communication, faster issue resolution, and improved service delivery.

Principles of Integrating ITSM with Agile and DevOps:

1. **Customer-Centricity**:

   - **Principle**: Prioritize customer needs and feedback throughout the service lifecycle.

2. **Iterative Development**:

   - **Principle**: Embrace iterative development cycles to respond to changing requirements and continuously improve services.

3. **Automation and Orchestration**:

   - **Principle**: Automate repetitive tasks and orchestrate workflows to streamline service delivery and minimize errors.

4. **Continuous Improvement**:

   - **Principle**: Foster a culture of continuous improvement across all teams involved, from development to operations to ITSM.

5. **Feedback Loops**:

- **Principle**: Establish feedback mechanisms to capture insights from stakeholders, driving continuous refinement of services.

Strategies for Integrating ITSM with Agile and DevOps:

1. **Communication and Collaboration**:

- **Strategy**: Promote open and transparent communication between development, operations, and ITSM teams to foster collaboration and shared ownership.

2. **Cross-Functional Teams**:

- **Strategy**: Form cross-functional teams that include members from development, operations, and ITSM to facilitate end-to-end service delivery.

3. **Common Toolsets**:

- **Strategy**: Implement common tools and platforms that support Agile, DevOps, and ITSM processes, enabling seamless integration.

4. **Agile Service Management**:

- **Strategy**: Apply Agile principles to ITSM processes,

allowing for faster response to incidents, changes, and service requests.

5. **Continuous Monitoring**:

   - **Strategy**: Implement continuous monitoring and performance measurement to ensure services meet quality and performance standards.

6. **Shared Metrics**:

   - **Strategy**: Define and track shared metrics that measure the effectiveness and efficiency of integrated processes.

Benefits of Integrating ITSM with Agile and DevOps:

1. **Faster Service Delivery**:

   - **Benefit**: Integration enables faster development and deployment of services, reducing time-to-market.

2. **Enhanced Service Quality**:

   - **Benefit**: Improved collaboration and automation result in higher service quality and fewer disruptions.

3. **Increased Efficiency**:

   - **Benefit**: Automation and streamlined processes reduce manual effort and resource wastage.

4. **Greater Adaptability**:

- **Benefit**: The integration supports better adaptability to changing business needs and technological advancements.

5. **Improved Customer Satisfaction**:

- **Benefit**: Agile and DevOps practices, combined with ITSM, result in services that better meet customer expectations.

In conclusion, the integration of ITSM with Agile and DevOps represents a holistic approach to service management that aligns IT with business goals, accelerates service delivery, and enhances quality. By fostering collaboration, embracing automation, and continuously improving processes, organizations can leverage the synergies of these disciplines to deliver IT services that drive business success and customer satisfaction. It's not just a convergence of methodologies; it's a strategic shift toward a more agile, responsive, and customer-centric ITSM approach.

C. Challenges and Opportunities in Modern IT Service Management (ITSM): Navigating the Digital Era

Modern ITSM is at the forefront of helping organizations harness technology to meet business goals and deliver exceptional services. However, with the rapid pace of technological change, there come both challenges and opportunities that shape the ITSM landscape. In this in-depth exploration, we will delve into the key challenges and opportunities in modern ITSM and how organizations can navigate this dynamic terrain.

Challenges in Modern ITSM:

1. **Rapid Technological Advancements**:

   - **Challenge**: The relentless pace of technological change requires ITSM to continually adapt to new tools, platforms, and methodologies.

2. **Complex Ecosystems**:

   - **Challenge**: Organizations often operate within complex IT ecosystems that involve hybrid cloud environments, third-party vendors, and interconnected services, making management more challenging.

3. **Data Security and Privacy**:

   - **Challenge**: Ensuring data security and compliance with privacy regulations, such as GDPR, remains a top concern for ITSM as cyber threats evolve.

4. **Service Availability and Reliability**:

   - **Challenge**: Maintaining high service availability and

reliability is essential, but it can be challenging with the increasing complexity of IT environments.

5. **Resource Constraints**:

   - **Challenge**: Many organizations face resource constraints, including budget limitations and talent shortages, which can hinder ITSM initiatives.

6. **Resistance to Change**:

   - **Challenge**: Employees and stakeholders may resist changes to established ITSM processes, slowing down the adoption of new methodologies.

Opportunities in Modern ITSM:

1. **Digital Transformation**:

   - **Opportunity**: Modern ITSM is a catalyst for digital transformation, enabling organizations to leverage technology for innovation, efficiency, and customer engagement.

2. **Automation and AI**:

   - **Opportunity**: The integration of automation and artificial intelligence in ITSM streamlines processes, reduces manual effort, and enhances service quality.

3. **Data-Driven Decision-Making**:

- **Opportunity**: Modern ITSM leverages data analytics to make informed decisions, optimize services, and improve customer experiences.

4. **Agile and DevOps Integration**:

- **Opportunity**: Integrating Agile and DevOps practices into ITSM allows for faster service delivery and better alignment with business objectives.

5. **Customer-Centricity**:

- **Opportunity**: Modern ITSM places a strong emphasis on understanding and meeting customer needs, resulting in higher customer satisfaction and loyalty.

6. **Service Innovation**:

- **Opportunity**: ITSM encourages service innovation, enabling organizations to stay competitive and seize new market opportunities.

Navigating the Challenges and Seizing Opportunities:

1. **Continuous Learning and Skill Development**:

- **Strategy**: Invest in training and skill development to keep ITSM teams updated on the latest technologies and best practices.

2. **Agile and DevOps Integration**:

   - **Strategy**: Embrace Agile and DevOps practices to accelerate service delivery and improve flexibility.

3. **Data Governance and Security**:

   - **Strategy**: Implement robust data governance and security measures to protect sensitive information and ensure compliance.

4. **Customer Engagement**:

   - **Strategy**: Foster strong relationships with customers and gather feedback to drive service improvements.

5. **Collaboration and Communication**:

   - **Strategy**: Promote collaboration and open communication between ITSM, development, and business teams.

6. **Automation and AI Adoption**:

   - **Strategy**: Identify areas where automation and AI can enhance ITSM processes and streamline operations.

In conclusion, modern ITSM is a dynamic and evolving field that presents both challenges and opportunities. By embracing new technologies, fostering a culture of innovation, and prioritizing customer satisfaction, organizations can navigate the challenges and capitalize on the opportunities to excel in the digital era. ITSM is not just a support function; it's a strategic enabler that can drive business growth and success when approached with a forward-thinking mindset.

D. ITSM in a Cloud Environment: Navigating the Digital Transformation

The integration of IT Service Management (ITSM) with cloud computing is a transformative journey that has redefined the way organizations deliver and manage IT services. Cloud environments offer unprecedented scalability, flexibility, and cost-efficiency, but they also present unique challenges in terms of governance, security, and service delivery. In this in-depth exploration, we'll delve into the significance, challenges, strategies, and best practices for implementing ITSM in a cloud environment.

Significance of ITSM in a Cloud Environment:

1. **Scalability and Flexibility**:

   - **Significance**: Cloud environments allow organizations to scale their IT resources up or down based on demand, enhancing agility and cost-efficiency.

2. **Resource Optimization**:

- **Significance**: ITSM in the cloud enables organizations to optimize resource allocation, reducing waste and improving efficiency.

3. **Rapid Service Deployment**:

- **Significance**: Cloud-based services can be deployed rapidly, enabling ITSM to respond quickly to changing business needs.

4. **Cost Control**:

- **Significance**: ITSM in the cloud provides cost control mechanisms, ensuring organizations only pay for the resources they use.

5. **Innovation**:

- **Significance**: Cloud environments foster innovation by providing access to cutting-edge technologies and services.

Challenges of ITSM in a Cloud Environment:

1. **Security and Compliance**:

- **Challenge**: Ensuring data security and compliance in a shared cloud environment requires robust policies and controls.

2. **Integration Complexity**:

   - **Challenge**: Integrating cloud services with existing ITSM processes and tools can be complex and require careful planning.

3. **Service Visibility**:

   - **Challenge**: Maintaining visibility and control over services in the cloud can be challenging, leading to potential service disruptions.

4. **Cost Management**:

   - **Challenge**: While cloud environments offer cost benefits, mismanagement can lead to unexpected expenses.

5. **Service Performance**:

   - **Challenge**: Ensuring consistent service performance in a dynamic cloud environment requires monitoring and optimization.

Strategies for Successful ITSM in a Cloud Environment:

1. **Cloud Governance**:

   - **Strategy**: Establish robust cloud governance policies

and controls to ensure security, compliance, and cost management.

2. **Integration Frameworks**:

   - **Strategy**: Implement integration frameworks that facilitate seamless communication between on-premises and cloud-based services.

3. **Service Catalog Management**:

   - **Strategy**: Maintain a well-defined service catalog that includes cloud services, ensuring transparency and control.

4. **Automation and Orchestration**:

   - **Strategy**: Leverage automation and orchestration to streamline cloud provisioning, scaling, and management.

5. **Cost Visibility**:

   - **Strategy**: Implement cost management tools and practices to monitor and optimize cloud spending.

6. **Security Measures**:

   - **Strategy**: Employ robust security measures, including identity and access management, encryption, and threat detection, to safeguard data in the cloud.

Best Practices for ITSM in a Cloud Environment:

1. **Service Mapping**:

   - **Best Practice**: Create service maps that document the relationships and dependencies between on-premises and cloud-based services.

2. **Incident Response Planning**:

   - **Best Practice**: Develop incident response plans that address potential cloud-related issues and ensure minimal service disruption.

3. **Continuous Monitoring**:

   - **Best Practice**: Implement continuous monitoring of cloud services to identify and address performance and security issues proactively.

4. **Cost Allocation**:

   - **Best Practice**: Allocate cloud costs to specific business units or projects to promote accountability and cost control.

5. **User Training**:

   - **Best Practice**: Provide training to users and IT staff to ensure they understand cloud services and best practices for using them.

In conclusion, ITSM in a cloud environment represents a strategic shift in how organizations manage and deliver IT services. While it presents challenges, the benefits of scalability, flexibility, and cost-efficiency make it an essential component of modern IT service management. By adopting robust governance, integration, and security measures, organizations can leverage the power of the cloud to enhance service delivery, drive innovation, and remain competitive in the digital era.

E. Future Trends in IT Service Management (ITSM): Shaping the Next Era of Service Excellence

The field of IT Service Management (ITSM) is in a constant state of evolution, driven by technological advancements, changing business needs, and emerging best practices. As organizations continue to navigate the digital transformation, several compelling trends are shaping the future of ITSM. In this in-depth exploration, we'll delve into the most significant future trends in ITSM and how they are poised to redefine the landscape of service management.

1. AI and Automation Revolution:

- **Trend**: Artificial Intelligence (AI), Machine Learning (ML), and automation are set to revolutionize ITSM. These technologies will enable predictive analytics for issue resolution, chatbots for support, and automated service delivery, reducing manual effort and enhancing efficiency.

- **Significance**: AI-driven automation will free up ITSM teams to focus on more strategic tasks and provide faster, more accurate responses to user inquiries.

2. Service Experience and Customer-Centricity:

- **Trend**: ITSM is shifting its focus towards delivering an exceptional service experience. This trend emphasizes understanding and exceeding customer expectations, resulting in higher user satisfaction.

- **Significance**: Customer-centric ITSM ensures that services align with business objectives and provide tangible value to users, enhancing overall organizational performance.

3. Service Integration and Ecosystems:

- **Trend**: Organizations are increasingly relying on complex service ecosystems involving multiple providers and platforms. Service Integration and Management (SIAM) is emerging as a key trend to manage these intricate relationships effectively.

- **Significance**: SIAM helps organizations maintain control, visibility, and coordination over diverse services, ensuring seamless service delivery.

4. Hybrid and Multi-Cloud Management:

- **Trend**: The adoption of hybrid and multi-cloud environments is on the rise. Managing services across these environments poses unique challenges related to governance, integration, and performance.

- **Significance**: ITSM will need to adapt to efficiently manage services in multi-cloud environments while ensuring security, compliance, and cost control.

5. Shift-left and Self-Service:

- **Trend**: The "shift-left" approach involves moving responsibilities and tasks closer to the user. Self-service portals, knowledge bases, and automation empower users to solve issues independently.

- **Significance**: This trend reduces the workload on ITSM teams, decreases resolution times, and improves user empowerment.

6. ITSM Beyond ITIL:

- **Trend**: While ITIL remains a foundational framework, ITSM is expanding beyond its confines. Organizations are integrating Agile, DevOps, Lean, and other practices into ITSM for more flexibility and agility.

- **Significance**: This trend allows organizations to align ITSM more closely with development, deliver services faster, and adapt to changing business needs.

7. Data-Driven Decision-Making:

- **Trend**: Data analytics and real-time monitoring are becoming integral to ITSM. Insights derived from data help in proactive problem-solving, resource optimization, and trend analysis.

- **Significance**: Data-driven ITSM enables informed decision-making, faster issue resolution, and better service performance.

8. Blockchain for ITSM:

- **Trend**: Blockchain technology is gaining traction in ITSM for enhancing security, traceability, and transparency in service management.

- **Significance**: Blockchain can be used to securely manage assets, track changes, and ensure data integrity within ITSM processes.

9. Robotic Process Automation (RPA) in ITSM:

- **Trend**: RPA is being employed to automate routine, rule-based ITSM tasks such as incident logging, password resets, and software deployments.

- **Significance**: RPA reduces manual effort, minimizes errors, and improves service efficiency.

10. Quantum Computing Implications:

Trend: While still in its infancy, quantum computing has the potential to revolutionize ITSM by solving complex problems and optimizing resource allocation in ways classical computing cannot.

Significance: Quantum computing may open new frontiers in ITSM, particularly in the realms of optimization, security, and data analysis.

In conclusion, the future of ITSM is marked by profound changes driven by technological innovations, changing customer expectations, and the need for greater agility and efficiency. Embracing these trends will empower organizations to deliver superior service experiences, remain competitive, and navigate the evolving digital landscape with confidence. ITSM is not merely adapting to change; it is leading the charge in shaping the future of service excellence.

CHAPTER 9

ITSM Tools and Technology

In the fast-paced and dynamic world of IT Service Management (ITSM), the role of tools and technology cannot be overstated. These essential resources have evolved from being mere enablers to becoming the driving force behind efficient and effective service delivery. In this introductory exploration, we'll embark on a journey into the realm of ITSM tools and technology, discovering their significance, impact, and how they empower organizations to achieve service excellence in the digital age.

The landscape of ITSM is constantly evolving, driven by the ever-increasing complexity of IT environments, the rising expectations of customers and users, and the need for organizations to stay competitive in an interconnected world. ITSM tools and technology are at the forefront of this evolution, offering innovative solutions to address the challenges and opportunities presented by the modern IT landscape.

Join us as we delve deeper into the world of ITSM tools and technology, where we'll explore the wide array of tools available, their role in optimizing ITSM processes, and the transformative potential they hold for organizations seeking to deliver seamless and exceptional IT services. From incident management and change control to automation and artificial intelligence, the tools and technology in ITSM are the catalysts for success in the digital era, empowering organizations to meet and exceed the expectations of their users and customers.

A. ITSM Software and Solutions: The Backbone of Service Management

IT Service Management (ITSM) software and solutions serve as the linchpin for organizations striving to deliver efficient, customer-centric IT services in today's digital landscape. These tools have evolved far beyond their initial purpose, becoming comprehensive platforms that streamline processes, enhance collaboration, and ensure IT services align with business objectives. In this in-depth exploration, we'll delve into the world of ITSM software and solutions, understanding their significance, key features, and the pivotal role they play in modern service management.

Significance of ITSM Software and Solutions:

1. **Centralized Service Management**:

   - **Significance**: ITSM software provides a centralized platform for managing IT services, enabling organizations to streamline processes and ensure consistency.

2. **Improved Efficiency**:

   - **Significance**: These tools automate routine tasks, reducing manual effort and enabling IT teams to allocate resources more effectively.

3. **Enhanced User Experience**:

   - **Significance**: ITSM solutions prioritize the user experience, offering self-service portals, knowledge bases, and efficient incident resolution.

4. **Change Control**:

   - **Significance**: ITSM software ensures that changes are managed and tracked effectively, reducing the risk of disruptions to services.

5. **Compliance and Reporting**:

   - **Significance**: These solutions provide tools for tracking and reporting on compliance with IT policies and industry regulations.

Key Features of ITSM Software and Solutions:

1. **Incident Management**:

   - **Feature**: ITSM software allows for the efficient

logging, tracking, and resolution of incidents, ensuring minimal service disruption.

2. **Change Management**:

   • **Feature**: Organizations can manage changes to IT services, applications, and infrastructure while minimizing risk.

3. **Service Catalog**:

   • **Feature**: ITSM solutions offer a service catalog that defines available services and enables users to request them through self-service portals.

4. **Asset Management**:

   • **Feature**: These tools help organizations track and manage IT assets, optimizing resource utilization.

5. **Knowledge Management**:

   • **Feature**: Knowledge bases store information, troubleshooting guides, and best practices, empowering users and support teams to find solutions quickly.

6. **Automation**:

   • **Feature**: Automation capabilities streamline

processes, reducing manual intervention and ensuring consistent service delivery.

7. **Reporting and Analytics**:

- **Feature**: ITSM solutions provide robust reporting and analytics tools for tracking service performance, compliance, and improvement opportunities.

Challenges in Implementing ITSM Software and Solutions:

1. **Complexity and Customization**:

- **Challenge**: Implementing ITSM solutions can be complex and may require customization to meet the specific needs of an organization.

2. **Change Management**:

- **Challenge**: Overcoming resistance to change from IT teams and end-users is a common challenge during implementation.

3. **Integration**:

- **Challenge**: Integrating ITSM software with existing systems and tools can be challenging, especially in heterogeneous IT environments.

4. **Costs**:

- **Challenge**: Licensing and implementation costs can be a barrier for some organizations, especially smaller ones.

5. **User Adoption**:

- **Challenge**: Ensuring that users and IT teams embrace and effectively utilize the ITSM software can be a challenge.

Best Practices for ITSM Software Implementation:

1. **Clearly Define Objectives**:

- **Best Practice**: Define clear objectives and outcomes for the ITSM implementation to ensure alignment with business goals.

2. **Involve Stakeholders**:

- **Best Practice**: Involve IT teams, end-users, and other relevant stakeholders in the selection and implementation process.

3. **Comprehensive Training**:

- **Best Practice**: Provide training and support to users and IT teams to ensure effective adoption of the ITSM software.

4. **Robust Change Management**:

  - **Best Practice**: Implement a change management strategy to address resistance and ensure smooth adoption.

5. **Regular Evaluation**:

  - **Best Practice**: Continuously evaluate the performance of the ITSM software and make improvements as needed.

In conclusion, ITSM software and solutions are the backbone of modern service management, enabling organizations to deliver efficient, user-centric IT services. While implementation may pose challenges, the benefits of improved efficiency, user satisfaction, and alignment with business objectives make these tools indispensable in today's digital era. When implemented thoughtfully and with a focus on user adoption, ITSM software empowers organizations to excel in service delivery and meet the ever-evolving demands of the digital landscape.

B. Configuration Management Databases (CMDBs): Orchestrating IT Service Control

Configuration Management Databases (CMDBs) are the

central repositories that underpin effective IT Service Management (ITSM). These databases store vital information about an organization's IT assets, infrastructure, and services, enabling precise control, efficient incident resolution, and informed decision-making. In this in-depth exploration, we'll delve into the world of CMDBs, understanding their significance, components, best practices, and their pivotal role in modern ITSM.

Significance of CMDBs:

1. **Holistic Visibility**:

   - **Significance**: CMDBs offer a holistic view of an organization's IT environment, including hardware, software, configurations, and relationships. This visibility is crucial for effective management and troubleshooting.

2. **Change Control**:

   - **Significance**: CMDBs track changes to configuration items (CIs) and their dependencies, ensuring that changes are managed, approved, and assessed for impact, reducing the risk of service disruptions.

3. **Incident and Problem Resolution**:

   - **Significance**: Accurate CMDB data streamlines

incident and problem resolution by providing support teams with up-to-date information on the affected CIs and their relationships.

4. **Service Mapping**:

   - **Significance**: CMDBs enable organizations to create service maps that illustrate how CIs interact to deliver IT services, facilitating service management and optimization.

5. **Risk Management**:

   - **Significance**: CMDBs support risk assessment by identifying vulnerabilities, dependencies, and potential impacts of changes or incidents.

Components of CMDBs:

1. **Configuration Items (CIs)**:

   - **Component**: The core elements of a CMDB, CIs represent IT assets, such as servers, software, networks, and more. They are categorized and organized within the CMDB.

2. **Relationships**:

   - **Component**: Relationships define the connections and dependencies between CIs. Understanding these relationships is crucial for change management and incident resolution.

3. **Attributes and Attributes Sets**:

   - **Component**: Attributes are properties or characteristics of CIs, such as specifications, versions, and locations. Attributes sets group related attributes for specific types of CIs.

4. **Data Models and Schema**:

   - **Component**: CMDBs use data models and schema to define how data is structured and stored within the database.

5. **User Interfaces**:

   - **Component**: CMDBs provide user interfaces for data input, visualization, and reporting. These interfaces are critical for users to interact with CMDB data.

Best Practices for CMDB Implementation:

1. **Clearly Define Scope**:

   - **Best Practice**: Clearly define the scope of the CMDB to ensure that it includes only relevant CIs and relationships.

2. **Data Accuracy and Validation**:

   - **Best Practice**: Implement processes for data validation and accuracy to ensure that the CMDB remains a reliable source of information.

3. **Change Management Integration**:

   - **Best Practice**: Integrate the CMDB with change management processes to assess the impact of proposed changes accurately.

4. **Automation and Discovery Tools**:

   - **Best Practice**: Implement automation and discovery tools to populate and update CMDB data, reducing manual effort and errors.

5. **Regular Auditing**:

   - **Best Practice**: Conduct regular audits to verify that the CMDB data aligns with the actual IT environment.

Challenges in CMDB Implementation:

1. **Data Quality**:

   - **Challenge**: Maintaining accurate and up-to-date CMDB data can be challenging, especially in large and dynamic IT environments.

2. **Integration Complexity**:

   - **Challenge**: Integrating CMDBs with other ITSM tools and systems requires careful planning and execution.

3. **Change Management Adoption**:

   - **Challenge**: Ensuring that IT teams adopt change management processes that rely on CMDB data can be challenging.

4. **Scalability**:

   - **Challenge**: As IT environments grow, scaling CMDBs to accommodate increasing numbers of CIs and relationships can be complex.

CMDBs in Modern ITSM:

In conclusion, CMDBs are fundamental to modern ITSM, offering organizations a centralized, accurate, and comprehensive view of their IT environment. When implemented and maintained effectively, CMDBs enable efficient incident resolution, change management, and service optimization. They are not just databases; they are critical tools that empower organizations to orchestrate IT service control, mitigate risks, and enhance service delivery in the ever-evolving world of technology.

C. Automation in ITSM: Revolutionizing Service Management

Automation in IT Service Management (ITSM) has emerged as a transformative force, reshaping how organizations deliver, manage, and optimize IT services. By automating routine tasks, workflows, and processes, automation not only accelerates service delivery but also enhances accuracy, reduces costs, and empowers IT teams to focus on strategic initiatives. In this in-depth exploration, we'll delve into the world of automation in ITSM, understanding its significance, key components, benefits, challenges, and best practices.

Significance of Automation in ITSM:

1. **Efficiency and Speed**:

   - **Significance**: Automation streamlines repetitive tasks and workflows, leading to faster incident resolution, request fulfillment, and service delivery.

2. **Accuracy and Consistency**:

   - **Significance**: Automated processes ensure consistency and reduce the risk of errors, leading to improved service quality.

3. **Cost Reduction**:

   - **Significance**: By reducing manual effort and

minimizing downtime, automation lowers operational costs and increases resource utilization.

4. **Enhanced User Experience**:

   - **Significance**: Automation provides users with self-service options, improving their experience by enabling quick access to services and support.

5. **Resource Allocation**:

   - **Significance**: IT teams can redirect their efforts from routine tasks to strategic initiatives, such as innovation and optimization.

Key Components of Automation in ITSM:

1. **Workflow Automation**:

   - **Component**: Workflow automation tools enable the creation of custom workflows for incident management, change management, and other ITSM processes.

2. **Orchestration**:

   - **Component**: Orchestration tools automate end-to-end processes by integrating various systems and applications.

3. **Scripting and Script Automation**:

   - **Component**: Scripting languages and automation scripts automate specific tasks or configurations.

4. **Chatbots and Virtual Agents**:

   - **Component**: Chatbots and virtual agents provide self-service options, answering user queries and performing tasks autonomously.

5. **Machine Learning and AI**:

   - **Component**: Machine learning and AI algorithms enable predictive analytics, anomaly detection, and proactive problem resolution.

Benefits of Automation in ITSM:

1. **Reduced Workload**:

   - **Benefit**: Automation handles routine tasks, reducing the workload on IT teams and minimizing human error.

2. **Faster Incident Resolution**:

   - **Benefit**: Automated incident management processes ensure rapid detection and resolution of issues, minimizing downtime.

3. **Cost Savings**:

   - **Benefit**: By optimizing resource utilization and reducing manual effort, automation leads to significant cost savings.

4. **Improved Compliance**:

   - **Benefit**: Automated change control and compliance checks enhance adherence to IT policies and regulatory requirements.

5. **Enhanced User Satisfaction**:

   - **Benefit**: Self-service options and quick service delivery improve the user experience and satisfaction.

Challenges in Implementing Automation in ITSM:

1. **Complexity**:

   - **Challenge**: Implementing automation can be complex, especially when integrating with existing ITSM processes and systems.

2. **Resistance to Change**:

   - **Challenge**: IT teams and users may resist automation, fearing job displacement or changes to familiar processes.

3. **Skill Gaps**:

   - **Challenge**: Organizations may lack the necessary skills and expertise to implement and manage automation effectively.

Best Practices for Implementing Automation in ITSM:

1. **Start Small**:

   - **Best Practice**: Begin with automating small, repetitive tasks and gradually expand automation initiatives.

2. **Collaboration**:

   - **Best Practice**: Involve IT teams, stakeholders, and end-users in the automation planning and implementation process.

3. **Education and Training**:

   - **Best Practice**: Provide training and resources to IT staff to build the skills required for automation.

4. **Monitoring and Optimization**:

   - **Best Practice**: Continuously monitor automated processes and workflows to identify opportunities for improvement.

5. **Change Management**:

- **Best Practice**: Implement a change management strategy to address resistance and ensure the successful adoption of automation.

In conclusion, automation in ITSM is a powerful catalyst for improving service management, driving efficiency, and enhancing user satisfaction. When carefully planned, implemented, and managed, automation not only optimizes ITSM processes but also positions organizations to excel in the ever-evolving digital landscape. It empowers IT teams to focus on innovation and strategic initiatives, ultimately contributing to the success of the organization. Automation is not merely a tool; it's a pivotal force in reshaping the future of IT service management.

D. AI and Machine Learning in ITSM: The Intelligent Transformation

Artificial Intelligence (AI) and Machine Learning (ML) have revolutionized the landscape of IT Service Management (ITSM) by infusing intelligence, automation, and data-driven decision-making into service delivery and support processes. These technologies enable organizations to predict, prevent, and resolve issues more efficiently, enhance the user experience, and drive continuous improvement. In this in-depth exploration, we'll dive into the world of AI and ML in ITSM, understanding their

Mastering IT Service Management and Infrastructure Library significance, applications, benefits, challenges, and best practices.

Significance of AI and Machine Learning in ITSM:

1. **Predictive Analytics**:

   - **Significance**: AI and ML algorithms analyze historical data to predict potential issues or outages, allowing proactive problem resolution and minimizing service disruptions.

2. **Automation and Chatbots**:

   - **Significance**: AI-driven automation, including chatbots and virtual agents, enables self-service, reducing the workload on IT teams and improving user satisfaction.

3. **Efficient Incident Management**:

   - **Significance**: AI can classify, prioritize, and assign incidents, streamlining the resolution process and reducing response times.

4. **Anomaly Detection**:

   - **Significance**: ML algorithms identify anomalies in system behavior, helping organizations detect security threats and performance issues.

5. **Personalized User Experience**:

- **Significance**: AI-driven personalization tailors IT services to individual user preferences and needs, enhancing the user experience.

Applications of AI and Machine Learning in ITSM:

1. **Predictive Maintenance**:

- **Application**: AI predicts when IT assets or infrastructure components are likely to fail, enabling proactive maintenance and minimizing downtime.

2. **Chatbots and Virtual Agents**:

- **Application**: AI-powered chatbots assist users with incident reporting, request fulfillment, and knowledge access, improving user support.

3. **Intelligent Routing**:

- **Application**: ML algorithms route incidents and requests to the most appropriate IT teams or specialists based on historical data and content analysis.

4. **Automation of Routine Tasks**:

- **Application**: AI automates routine, repetitive tasks, such as password resets and software deployments, freeing up IT staff for more strategic work.

5. **Natural Language Processing (NLP)**:

- **Application**: NLP enables AI systems to understand and respond to user queries in natural language, enhancing the user experience.

Benefits of AI and Machine Learning in ITSM:

1. **Efficiency and Productivity**:

- **Benefit**: AI-driven automation reduces manual effort, increasing IT team productivity and service delivery efficiency.

2. **Proactive Issue Resolution**:

- **Benefit**: Predictive analytics and anomaly detection enable organizations to address issues before they impact users, minimizing disruptions.

3. **Cost Reduction**:

- **Benefit**: AI and ML optimization reduces operational costs and resource allocation by streamlining processes and preventing incidents.

4. **Enhanced User Experience**:

- **Benefit**: Chatbots and personalized services improve

the user experience by providing quick, tailored support.

5. **Data-Driven Decision-Making**:

- **Benefit**: AI and ML provide actionable insights from data, enabling informed decisions and strategic planning.

Challenges in Implementing AI and Machine Learning in ITSM:

1. **Data Quality and Availability**:

- **Challenge**: Implementing AI and ML requires high-quality, accessible data, which can be a challenge for some organizations.

2. **Integration Complexity**:

- **Challenge**: Integrating AI and ML solutions with existing ITSM tools and processes can be complex.

3. **Skill Gap**:

- **Challenge**: Organizations may lack the skills and expertise required to implement and manage AI and ML effectively.

Best Practices for Implementing AI and Machine Learning in ITSM:

1. **Start Small and Iterate**:

   - **Best Practice**: Begin with small, well-defined AI/ML projects and expand as you gain experience and confidence.

2. **Data Governance**:

   - **Best Practice**: Establish data governance practices to ensure data quality, security, and accessibility.

3. **Collaboration and Training**:

   - **Best Practice**: Foster collaboration between IT and data science teams, providing training and resources to build AI/ML expertise.

4. **Ethical Considerations**:

   - **Best Practice**: Consider ethical and privacy implications when implementing AI and ML, ensuring compliance with regulations.

In conclusion, AI and Machine Learning are propelling ITSM into an era of intelligent, data-driven service management. When strategically implemented and managed, these technologies empower organizations to deliver superior IT services, improve efficiency, reduce costs, and enhance the user experience. As AI and ML continue to advance, their role in ITSM will become increasingly pivotal, enabling organizations to navigate the complexities of the digital landscape with agility and intelligence.

E. Evaluating and Choosing ITSM Tools: Your Path to Service Excellence

Selecting the right IT Service Management (ITSM) tools is a critical decision for organizations aiming to streamline service delivery, enhance user satisfaction, and optimize IT processes. The evaluation and selection process should be thorough and strategic to ensure that the chosen tools align with your organization's unique needs and goals. In this in-depth exploration, we'll delve into the world of evaluating and choosing ITSM tools, understanding the significance, key considerations, challenges, and best practices.

Significance of Evaluating and Choosing ITSM Tools:

1. **Service Efficiency and Effectiveness**:

   - **Significance**: The right ITSM tools streamline processes, reduce manual effort, and enhance efficiency, ultimately improving service delivery.

2. **User Satisfaction**:

- **Significance**: Tools that empower self-service and provide a seamless user experience contribute to higher user satisfaction.

3. **Cost Optimization**:

- **Significance**: Choosing cost-effective tools that align with your organization's budget helps optimize ITSM operations.

4. **Alignment with Objectives**:

- **Significance**: Tools should align with your organization's specific ITSM objectives, whether it's compliance, automation, or improved incident management.

Key Considerations for Evaluating and Choosing ITSM Tools:

1. **Requirements Gathering**:

- **Consideration**: Thoroughly define your organization's ITSM requirements, considering factors like scalability, integration capabilities, and specific functionality needed.

2. **Budget Constraints**:

- **Consideration**: Determine your budget for ITSM tools and seek solutions that provide value within your financial constraints.

3. **Scalability**:

- **Consideration**: Assess whether the tools can scale with your organization's growth and evolving IT needs.

4. **Integration Capabilities**:

- **Consideration**: Evaluate how well the ITSM tools can integrate with your existing IT infrastructure, including other tools and systems.

5. **User Experience**:

- **Consideration**: Ensure that the tools offer a user-friendly interface and self-service capabilities to enhance the user experience.

6. **Vendor Reputation**:

- **Consideration**: Research and assess the reputation and track record of ITSM tool vendors, including customer reviews and references.

Challenges in Evaluating and Choosing ITSM Tools:

1. **Overwhelm with Choices**:

    -   **Challenge**: The abundance of ITSM tool options in the market can be overwhelming, making it challenging to make a selection.

2. **Complexity of Requirements**:

    -   **Challenge**: Organizations with complex ITSM needs may struggle to find a tool that aligns perfectly with their requirements.

3. **Vendor Lock-In**:

    -   **Challenge**: Selecting a tool that isn't easily replaceable can result in vendor lock-in, limiting future flexibility.

Best Practices for Evaluating and Choosing ITSM Tools:

1. **Cross-Functional Team**:

    -   **Best Practice**: Form a cross-functional evaluation team that includes IT, business, and user representatives to ensure diverse perspectives.

2. **Pilot Testing**:

    -   **Best Practice**: Conduct pilot tests to evaluate how the tools perform in real-world scenarios and gather feedback from users.

3. **Request for Proposal (RFP)**:

   - **Best Practice**: Use RFPs to solicit detailed information from vendors, helping you make informed decisions.

4. **Scoring Criteria**:

   - **Best Practice**: Create a scoring system that quantifies the alignment of each tool with your requirements, facilitating an objective evaluation.

5. **Consult Peers and Experts**:

   - **Best Practice**: Seek advice and recommendations from industry peers, consultants, or experts who have experience with ITSM tools.

6. **Consider Future Needs**:

   - **Best Practice**: Ensure that the selected tool aligns with your organization's future ITSM needs, allowing for scalability and adaptability.

In conclusion, evaluating and choosing ITSM tools is a crucial step in achieving service excellence and IT operational efficiency. By following a systematic and thorough evaluation process, aligning tools with specific requirements, and considering factors like user experience and integration capabilities, organizations can select tools that empower them to meet their ITSM objectives and deliver superior IT services. It's a journey that, when executed with care and strategy, can lead to transformative improvements in IT service management.

CHAPTER 10

Case Studies and Success Stories

Within the realm of IT Service Management (ITSM), the true measure of success often lies in the tangible results and real-world transformations achieved by organizations. Case studies and success stories serve as windows into these remarkable journeys, offering insights into how ITSM strategies, methodologies, and tools can create substantial value. In this introductory exploration, we embark on a journey into the world of case studies and success stories, where we unveil the practical impact of ITSM and ITIL implementation, industry-specific challenges overcome, innovations embraced, and valuable lessons learned.

ITSM isn't just a theoretical concept; it's a dynamic discipline that adapts to the unique needs and challenges of organizations across various sectors. Case studies and success stories showcase how ITSM practices have been tailored to address specific industry requirements, compliance standards, and customer expectations.

Join us on this expedition as we delve deeper into these stories of ITSM triumphs and how they have reshaped organizations, optimized services, enhanced customer experiences, and, ultimately, driven success. From healthcare to finance, manufacturing to technology, these case studies illuminate the power of ITSM to transform businesses and elevate them to new heights.

These narratives are more than just success stories; they are blueprints for organizations seeking to harness the potential of ITSM and ITIL to overcome obstacles, innovate, and excel in today's rapidly evolving digital landscape. Each case study is a testament to the transformative capabilities of ITSM, demonstrating how it can turn challenges into opportunities and pave the way for a brighter future in the world of IT service management.

A. Real-World Implementations of ITSM and ITIL: Transforming Organizations for Success

Real-world implementations of IT Service Management (ITSM) and ITIL (Information Technology Infrastructure Library) provide tangible evidence of the profound impact these methodologies can have on organizations across industries. They demonstrate how ITSM and ITIL frameworks, practices, and principles are not merely theoretical concepts but powerful tools that enable businesses to optimize their IT services, enhance operational efficiency, and drive business success. In this in-depth exploration, we'll delve into several real-world implementations of ITSM and ITIL, examining their significance, key takeaways, and the transformative effects they've had on organizations.

Significance of Real-World ITSM and ITIL Implementations:

1. **Operational Excellence**:

   - **Significance**: Successful ITSM and ITIL implementations lead to operational excellence by establishing standardized processes, efficient service delivery, and improved resource utilization.

2. **Service Quality**:

   - **Significance**: These implementations focus on delivering high-quality IT services that align with business objectives and meet customer expectations.

3. **Cost Reduction**:

   - **Significance**: Implementing ITSM and ITIL often results in cost reduction through improved resource management and reduced incidents and outages.

4. **Compliance and Risk Management**:

   - **Significance**: These frameworks help organizations ensure compliance with industry regulations, minimize risks, and enhance security.

5. **Customer Satisfaction**:

- **Significance**: Real-world implementations prioritize the user experience, leading to increased customer and end-user satisfaction.

Key Takeaways from Real-World Implementations:

1. **Process Standardization**:

- **Takeaway**: Successful implementations emphasize the standardization of IT processes, from incident and change management to service request fulfillment.

2. **Continuous Improvement**:

- **Takeaway**: ITSM and ITIL encourage a culture of continuous improvement, with organizations regularly reviewing and optimizing their processes.

3. **Efficient Incident Management**:

- **Takeaway**: Implementations enable organizations to respond to and resolve incidents more efficiently, minimizing service disruptions.

4. **Service Catalog Implementation**:

- **Takeaway**: Organizations often establish service catalogs that define available services and enable end-users to request them through self-service portals.

5. **Change Control and Governance**:

   - **Takeaway**: Real-world implementations prioritize change control and governance, ensuring that changes are managed and approved in a structured manner.

Transformative Effects of Real-World Implementations:

1. **Healthcare Sector Transformation**:

   - **Example**: A healthcare organization implemented ITSM and ITIL to streamline its IT services. The result was reduced downtime, faster incident resolution, and improved patient care.

2. **Financial Services Excellence**:

   - **Example**: A financial institution leveraged ITSM and ITIL to enhance security, manage risk, and achieve regulatory compliance while reducing operational costs.

3. **Manufacturing Efficiency**:

   - **Example**: A manufacturing company optimized its IT services through ITSM, leading to improved production processes, reduced downtime, and significant cost savings.

4. **Technology Sector Innovation**:

- **Example**: A technology company used ITSM and ITIL to drive innovation, enabling it to rapidly develop and deploy new services, products, and features.

5. **Government Service Enhancement**:

- **Example**: A government agency adopted ITSM and ITIL to improve citizen services, resulting in more efficient and responsive government operations.

These real-world implementations of ITSM and ITIL serve as inspiring success stories that showcase the transformative potential of these frameworks. They underscore the adaptability of ITSM and ITIL to diverse industries and the substantial benefits organizations can achieve by implementing best practices, standardizing processes, and prioritizing the user experience. Through these implementations, businesses have not only overcome challenges but also positioned themselves for sustained growth, innovation, and success in the ever-evolving landscape of IT service management.

B. Industry-specific Case Studies: Tailoring ITSM and ITIL for Success

Industry-specific case studies offer a unique perspective on how organizations within various sectors have customized and applied IT Service Management (ITSM) and ITIL (Information Technology Infrastructure Library) frameworks to address their distinct challenges, compliance requirements, and operational goals. These real-world examples illustrate the versatility of ITSM and ITIL, showcasing how they can be adapted to deliver industry-specific benefits and drive excellence. In this in-depth exploration, we'll dive into industry-specific case studies, examining their significance, key takeaways, and the innovative approaches organizations have taken to leverage ITSM and ITIL.

Significance of Industry-specific Case Studies:

1. **Tailored Solutions**:

   - **Significance**: Industry-specific case studies demonstrate the capacity of ITSM and ITIL to be tailored to meet the unique needs and demands of different sectors.

2. **Compliance and Regulation**:

   - **Significance**: These studies highlight how organizations use ITSM and ITIL to ensure compliance with industry regulations, enhancing security and risk management.

3. **Operational Excellence**:

   - **Significance**: Implementations showcase how ITSM

and ITIL can drive operational excellence within specific industries, resulting in cost savings, process efficiency, and enhanced service quality.

4. **Innovation and Growth**:

   - **Significance**: Case studies often reveal how ITSM and ITIL enable organizations to innovate and position themselves for growth and competitiveness.

Key Takeaways from Industry-specific Case Studies:

1. **Sector-specific Processes**:

   - **Takeaway**: Industry-specific adaptations of ITSM and ITIL involve the incorporation of sector-specific processes and workflows.

2. **Regulatory Compliance**:

   - **Takeaway**: These implementations prioritize compliance with industry-specific regulations, ensuring that organizations meet legal and security requirements.

3. **Customized Service Offerings**:

   - **Takeaway**: ITSM and ITIL enable organizations to customize their service catalogs and offerings to align with industry-specific requirements.

4. **User Experience Enhancement**:

- **Takeaway**: Case studies often highlight improvements in the user experience, which is essential for sectors such as healthcare and government.

5. **Innovative Approaches**:

- **Takeaway**: Organizations in various industries innovate by leveraging ITSM and ITIL to develop new services, optimize existing ones, and enhance customer experiences.

Examples of Industry-specific Case Studies:

1. **Healthcare Excellence**:

- **Example**: A healthcare organization implemented ITSM and ITIL to standardize patient data management, resulting in improved data security, compliance with HIPAA regulations, and enhanced patient care.

2. **Financial Services Compliance**:

- **Example**: A financial services firm adopted ITSM and ITIL to ensure compliance with strict financial regulations, leading to streamlined auditing processes, reduced compliance risk, and improved customer trust.

3. **Manufacturing Efficiency**:

- **Example**: A manufacturing company used ITSM and ITIL to optimize its supply chain and production processes, resulting in reduced downtime, cost savings, and increased production efficiency.

4. **Retail Customer Experience**:

- **Example**: A retail chain embraced ITSM and ITIL to enhance the customer experience through personalized promotions and efficient order processing, resulting in increased sales and customer loyalty.

5. **Government Service Enhancement**:

- **Example**: A government agency implemented ITSM and ITIL to improve citizen services, enabling faster response times to inquiries and requests, and enhancing transparency and trust.

These industry-specific case studies illustrate how ITSM and ITIL can be adapted to address the unique challenges and objectives of various sectors. They serve as valuable guides for organizations seeking to optimize their IT services, adhere to industry regulations, and excel in delivering sector-specific value. Through these implementations, businesses have demonstrated the remarkable versatility of ITSM and ITIL in driving success across diverse industries.

C. Challenges Faced and Overcome in ITSM and ITIL Implementations: Paving the Path to Excellence

The journey of implementing IT Service Management (ITSM) and ITIL (Information Technology Infrastructure Library) in organizations is marked by both significant benefits and notable challenges. While these frameworks offer a structured approach to IT service delivery and management, the road to success can be riddled with obstacles that require careful navigation. In this in-depth exploration, we'll delve into the common challenges faced during ITSM and ITIL implementations, examining how organizations have overcome them to achieve operational excellence, compliance, and enhanced service quality.

Common Challenges Faced During ITSM and ITIL Implementations:

1. **Resistance to Change**:

    - **Challenge**: Employees and stakeholders may resist changes to established workflows and processes, fearing disruption and job role changes.

2. **Lack of Executive Support**:

   - **Challenge**: Without strong executive buy-in and support, ITSM and ITIL initiatives may lack the necessary resources and authority to succeed.

3. **Complexity of Implementation**:

   - **Challenge**: The complexity of ITSM and ITIL implementations, especially in large organizations, can overwhelm project teams and lead to delays and cost overruns.

4. **Data Quality and Availability**:

   - **Challenge**: Poor data quality and the unavailability of necessary data can hinder ITSM and ITIL efforts, especially in areas like asset management and incident analysis.

5. **Cultural Shift**:

   - **Challenge**: Shifting from a reactive to a proactive IT culture can be challenging, requiring changes in mindset and behavior.

Strategies for Overcoming Challenges in ITSM and ITIL Implementations:

1. **Change Management**:

   - **Strategy**: Implement a robust change management plan that includes communication, training, and stakeholder engagement to address resistance and build support.

2. **Executive Sponsorship**:

   - **Strategy**: Secure executive sponsorship early in the project to ensure commitment, allocate resources, and demonstrate leadership support.

3. **Phased Implementation**:

   - **Strategy**: Break down the implementation into manageable phases, starting with high-impact areas, to reduce complexity and minimize disruption.

4. **Data Governance**:

   - **Strategy**: Prioritize data quality and availability initiatives to ensure that accurate data is readily accessible for decision-making and reporting.

5. **Employee Training and Education**:

- **Strategy**: Invest in training and education programs to help employees adapt to new processes and foster a culture of continuous improvement.

Real-world Examples of Challenges Overcome:

1. **Resistance to Change in Healthcare**:

- **Example**: A healthcare organization faced resistance from medical staff when implementing ITSM and ITIL. They addressed this by involving doctors and nurses in process design and demonstrating how it would improve patient care.

2. **Executive Support in Finance**:

- **Example**: A financial services company struggled to secure executive support for ITIL adoption. They overcame this challenge by presenting a business case highlighting the potential cost savings and regulatory compliance benefits.

3. **Complexity in Manufacturing**:

- **Example**: A manufacturing company with a complex supply chain encountered implementation challenges. They tackled this by dividing the implementation into phases, starting with inventory management, and gradually expanding to other areas.

4. **Data Quality in Retail**:

   - **Example**: A retail chain found that inaccurate data hindered inventory management. They invested in data cleansing and validation processes before implementing ITSM and ITIL, ensuring data accuracy.

5. **Cultural Shift in Government**:

   - **Example**: A government agency needed to shift from a reactive to a proactive approach. They initiated cultural change workshops, encouraging employees to embrace proactive problem-solving and continuous improvement.

In conclusion, the successful implementation of ITSM and ITIL is not without its challenges, but organizations that navigate these obstacles effectively can reap substantial rewards in terms of operational efficiency, compliance, and service quality. By employing strategies such as change management, executive sponsorship, phased implementation, data governance, and employee training, organizations can overcome hurdles and pave the path to excellence in IT service management and delivery. These challenges, when conquered, become stepping stones to achieving the full potential of ITSM and ITIL.

D. Innovations and Lessons Learned in ITSM and ITIL Implementations: Forging a Path to Excellence

Implementing IT Service Management (ITSM) and ITIL (Information Technology Infrastructure Library) isn't just about adopting established best practices; it's also an opportunity for innovation and continuous improvement. Organizations that embark on this journey often uncover unique solutions to their challenges and valuable lessons that shape their future strategies. In this in-depth exploration, we'll delve into the innovations and key lessons learned during ITSM and ITIL implementations, examining their significance, real-world examples, and how they have contributed to enhanced service quality, efficiency, and effectiveness.

Significance of Innovations and Lessons Learned:

1. **Continuous Improvement Culture**:

   - **Significance**: Innovations and lessons learned foster a culture of continuous improvement, encouraging organizations to evolve and adapt.

2. **Efficiency and Effectiveness**:

   - **Significance**: Innovations often lead to enhanced efficiency and effectiveness in IT service delivery, reducing costs and service disruptions.

3. **Strategic Insights**:

- **Significance**: Lessons learned provide strategic insights that guide future initiatives and help organizations avoid common pitfalls.

4. **Competitive Advantage**:

- **Significance**: Innovative approaches and lessons learned can provide a competitive advantage by enabling organizations to deliver superior IT services.

Innovations and Lessons Learned in ITSM and ITIL Implementations:

1. **Automation for Efficiency**:

- **Innovation**: Organizations have innovated by implementing automation for routine tasks such as incident routing, password resets, and software deployment, leading to significant time and cost savings.

- **Lesson Learned**: Automation should be strategically planned and balanced with the need for human oversight, especially for critical tasks.

2. **Self-Service Portals**:

- **Innovation**: Self-service portals empower end-users to

resolve common issues and requests independently, reducing the workload on IT teams and enhancing the user experience.

- **Lesson Learned**: Effective self-service requires user-friendly interfaces and thorough knowledge bases.

3. **AI-powered Chatbots**:

- **Innovation**: AI-powered chatbots provide immediate support to end-users, improving response times and freeing IT staff for more complex tasks.

- **Lesson Learned**: Chatbots should be continually trained and updated to provide accurate and helpful responses.

4. **Data-Driven Decision-Making**:

- **Innovation**: Organizations have harnessed data analytics to make informed decisions, identify trends, and predict potential issues before they impact services.

- **Lesson Learned**: Data quality and accuracy are paramount for meaningful insights.

5. **DevOps Integration**:

- **Innovation**: Integrating ITSM with DevOps practices

has led to faster application development and deployment, enabling organizations to respond more swiftly to changing business needs.

- **Lesson Learned**: Collaboration and communication between ITSM and DevOps teams are essential for successful integration.

Real-world Examples of Innovations and Lessons Learned:

1. **Automation in Healthcare**:

   - **Innovation**: A healthcare organization automated appointment scheduling and reminders, reducing administrative workloads and improving patient satisfaction.

   - **Lesson Learned**: Effective automation requires careful consideration of patient privacy and data security.

2. **Self-Service in Finance**:

   - **Innovation**: A financial institution introduced self-service account management, allowing customers to handle routine transactions independently.

   - **Lesson Learned**: User education is crucial to ensure customers are comfortable with self-service options.

3. **Chatbots in Retail**:

- **Innovation**: A retail chain implemented AI-powered chatbots for customer support, leading to faster response times and increased online sales.

- **Lesson Learned**: Chatbot responses should be tailored to the context and customer queries.

4. **Data Analytics in Manufacturing**:

- **Innovation**: A manufacturing company used data analytics to optimize supply chain management, reducing costs and improving production efficiency.

- **Lesson Learned**: Data integrity and real-time data access are essential for accurate analytics.

5. **DevOps Integration in Technology**:

- **Innovation**: A technology company integrated ITSM and DevOps practices, resulting in faster software releases and improved responsiveness to customer demands.

- **Lesson Learned**: Collaboration between ITSM and DevOps teams requires strong communication and shared objectives.

In conclusion, innovations and lessons learned in ITSM and

ITIL implementations are the driving forces behind organizational growth and excellence in IT service management. By embracing automation, self-service, AI-powered solutions, data-driven decision-making, and DevOps integration, organizations can unlock new levels of efficiency and effectiveness. Additionally, the lessons learned from these innovations provide invaluable insights that guide future strategies and ensure continuous improvement. The dynamic nature of ITSM and ITIL allows organizations to adapt, innovate, and thrive in the ever-evolving landscape of IT service delivery.

Conclusion

As we draw the final curtain on this journey through these pages, we invite you to reflect on the knowledge, insights, and discoveries that have unfolded before you. Our exploration of various subjects has been a captivating voyage into the depths of understanding.

In these chapters, we have ventured through the intricacies of numerous topics and examined the key concepts and findings that define these fields. It is our hope that you have found inspiration, enlightenment, and valuable takeaways that resonate with you on your own quest for knowledge.

Remember that the pursuit of understanding is an ever-evolving journey, and this book is but a milestone along the way. The world of knowledge is vast and boundless, offering endless opportunities for exploration and growth.

As you conclude this book, we encourage you to carry forward the torch of curiosity and continue your exploration of these subjects. Seek out new perspectives, engage in meaningful discussions, and embrace the thrill of lifelong learning.

We express our sincere gratitude for joining us on this intellectual adventure. Your curiosity and dedication to expanding your horizons are the driving forces behind our shared quest for wisdom and insight.

Thank you for entrusting us with a portion of your intellectual journey. May your pursuit of knowledge lead you to new heights and inspire others to embark on their own quests for understanding.

With sincere appreciation,

Nikhilesh Mishra, Author

Recap of Key Takeaways

As we conclude our journey through the world of IT Service Management (ITSM) and ITIL (Information Technology Infrastructure Library), it's essential to recap and consolidate the key concepts that form the foundation of these frameworks. A comprehensive understanding of these concepts is crucial for organizations aiming to excel in IT service management and delivery. In this in-depth recap, we'll revisit the fundamental principles, processes, and components that make up ITSM and ITIL, reinforcing their significance and interplay.

Fundamental ITSM Concepts:

1. **Service**: Services are the core offerings of ITSM, addressing the needs of customers and users. They can be tangible (hardware) or intangible (software).

2. **Service Management**: Service management encompasses all activities related to planning, designing, delivering, and supporting IT services to meet business goals.

3. **Process**: Processes are structured activities that transform inputs into valuable outputs. ITSM relies on well-defined processes for efficient service delivery.

4. **Lifecycle Approach**: ITSM adopts a service lifecycle approach, consisting of service strategy, service design, service transition, service operation, and continual service improvement (CSI) stages.

Key ITIL Concepts:

1. **Service Strategy**: ITIL's service strategy stage focuses on aligning IT services with business objectives and ensuring that they provide value to the organization.

2. **Service Design**: This stage emphasizes the design of IT services, including service catalog management, service level management, capacity management, availability management, and IT service continuity management.

3. **Service Transition**: Service transition involves transitioning services from development to production environments while

managing changes, releases, and knowledge effectively.

4. **Service Operation**: Service operation ensures that IT services are delivered efficiently and effectively. It includes incident management, problem management, request fulfillment, event management, and access management.

5. **Continual Service Improvement (CSI)**: CSI is a fundamental concept in ITIL, promoting a culture of ongoing improvement through monitoring, measuring, and optimizing IT services and processes.

Components of ITIL:

1. **ITIL Service Value System (SVS)**: The SVS represents the overall model for how ITIL components work together to create value for organizations and customers.

2. **Guiding Principles**: ITIL's guiding principles, such as "Focus on Value" and "Collaborate and Promote Visibility," provide a foundation for decision-making and behavior within organizations.

3. **Four Dimensions of Service Management**: ITIL considers four dimensions—organizations and people, information and technology, partners and suppliers, and value streams and processes—as critical factors in service management.

Recap of Key ITSM and ITIL Principles:

1. **Customer Focus**: Both ITSM and ITIL emphasize aligning IT services with customer needs and ensuring customer satisfaction.

2. **Process Integration**: Effective process integration and coordination are essential for seamless service delivery and continuous improvement.

3. **Flexibility and Adaptability**: ITSM and ITIL stress the importance of flexibility to adapt to changing business requirements and technology advancements.

4. **Measurement and Metrics**: Metrics and Key Performance Indicators (KPIs) are used to measure the performance and effectiveness of IT services and processes.

5. **Continuous Improvement**: The culture of continual improvement is at the core of ITSM and ITIL, encouraging organizations to regularly assess and enhance their practices.

Recap of Key ITSM and ITIL Processes:

1. **Service Level Management**: Ensures that agreed-upon service levels are achieved and maintained.

2. **Change Management**: Manages changes to IT services in a controlled and efficient manner.

3. **Incident Management**: Focuses on restoring normal service operation as quickly as possible when incidents occur.

4. **Problem Management**: Identifies the root causes of incidents and prevents their recurrence.

5. **Request Fulfillment**: Handles service requests from users efficiently.

6. **Knowledge Management**: Captures, stores, and shares knowledge and information to support decision-making and problem-solving.

7. **Release and Deployment Management**: Ensures that new and changed services are delivered into the production environment smoothly.

8. **Capacity Management**: Ensures that IT resources are properly sized to meet current and future demands.

9. **Availability Management**: Maximizes the availability of IT services by reducing the impact of incidents and problems.

10. **IT Service Continuity Management**: Ensures that IT services can be restored quickly after a disaster or major disruption.

This recap serves as a comprehensive review of the key concepts, principles, and processes that underpin ITSM and ITIL. Organizations that embrace these concepts and apply them effectively are well-equipped to optimize their IT service management, align IT with business objectives, and deliver value to their customers and users. It's a journey of continual improvement and adaptability that positions organizations for success in the ever-evolving landscape of IT service delivery.

The Future of ITSM and ITIL

As the digital landscape continues to evolve at an unprecedented pace, IT Service Management (ITSM) and ITIL (Information Technology Infrastructure Library) are poised to play an increasingly vital role in shaping the future of IT service delivery. In this in-depth exploration, we'll delve into the emerging trends and transformative shifts that will define the future of ITSM and ITIL, ensuring organizations are prepared to navigate the path to digital excellence.

1. **Digital Transformation and ITSM**:

- **The Future**: ITSM will be at the forefront of digital transformation efforts, facilitating the integration of emerging technologies like artificial intelligence (AI), machine learning, Internet of Things (IoT), and automation to streamline operations and enhance service delivery.

- **Impact**: Organizations will leverage ITSM to align technology investments with business strategies, enabling rapid innovation, enhanced customer experiences, and competitive advantages.

2. **Shift to a Service-Centric Approach**:

- **The Future**: ITSM and ITIL will shift towards a more service-centric approach, focusing on delivering outcomes and experiences rather than just managing technology components.

- **Impact**: This shift will require organizations to reconfigure processes, tools, and mindsets to prioritize service value and customer satisfaction.

3. **AI and Automation Integration**:

- **The Future**: AI and automation will become integral to ITSM, handling routine tasks, predicting incidents, and automating complex processes.

- **Impact**: This integration will lead to faster incident resolution, improved efficiency, and the ability to proactively address issues before they impact service quality.

4. **Enhanced Data Analytics and Insights**:

- **The Future**: ITSM and ITIL will leverage advanced data analytics to gain deeper insights into service performance, trends, and customer preferences.

- **Impact**: Data-driven decision-making will drive improvements in service design, incident management, and problem resolution.

5. **Cloud and Hybrid Environments**:

- **The Future**: ITSM will adapt to manage services in cloud and hybrid environments, ensuring seamless integration and optimization.

- **Impact**: Organizations will need to balance agility with governance and security in these dynamic IT landscapes.

6. **Service Integration and Management (SIAM)**:

- **The Future**: SIAM will gain prominence as organizations manage an increasing number of external service providers and partners.

- **Impact**: SIAM will help ensure efficient coordination, integration, and governance of services from multiple sources.

7. Shift-left Approach to Support:

- **The Future**: Organizations will adopt a "shift-left" approach, empowering end-users to resolve more issues independently through self-service and knowledge management.

- **Impact**: This approach will reduce the burden on IT support teams, increase end-user satisfaction, and accelerate incident resolution.

8. Cybersecurity Integration:

- **The Future**: Cybersecurity will be tightly integrated with ITSM and ITIL to proactively identify and mitigate security threats.

- **Impact**: Organizations will enhance their security posture, protect sensitive data, and minimize service disruptions.

9. **Agility and DevOps Alignment**:

- **The Future**: ITSM and ITIL will align more closely with Agile and DevOps practices to enable faster development and delivery of IT services.

- **Impact**: This alignment will foster a culture of collaboration and continuous improvement, driving innovation and responsiveness.

10. **Robust Governance and Compliance**:

- **The Future**: ITSM and ITIL will continue to emphasize robust governance and compliance, especially in regulated industries.

- **Impact**: Organizations will reduce risk, meet compliance requirements, and build trust with customers and regulators.

In conclusion, the future of ITSM and ITIL is marked by adaptability, innovation, and a relentless focus on delivering value to organizations and their customers. As technology continues to advance, organizations that embrace these future trends and align their ITSM and ITIL practices accordingly will position themselves for success in the digital age. ITSM and ITIL will not just be frameworks; they will be the guiding principles that enable organizations to thrive in an ever-evolving, technology-driven world.

Glossary of Terms

To effectively navigate the world of IT Service Management (ITSM) and ITIL (Information Technology Infrastructure Library), it's essential to grasp the terminology that underpins these frameworks. This comprehensive glossary provides an in-depth explanation of key ITSM and ITIL terms, ensuring clarity and understanding as you embark on your journey toward IT service excellence.

1. Service:

- **Definition**: A means of delivering value to customers by facilitating outcomes they want to achieve, without the ownership of specific costs and risks.

2. Service Management:

- **Definition**: A set of specialized organizational capabilities for delivering value to customers in the form of services.

3. Process:

- **Definition**: A structured set of activities designed to accomplish a specific objective. In ITSM, processes are key for efficient service delivery.

4. Incident:

- **Definition**: An unplanned interruption or reduction in the quality of an IT service. Incident management focuses on restoring normal service operation quickly.

5. Problem:

- **Definition**: The root cause or underlying issue of one or more incidents. Problem management seeks to identify and address these root causes.

6. Change Management:

- **Definition**: The process of controlling changes to the IT environment, ensuring they are well-planned, minimize risks, and have the desired outcomes.

7. Service Level Agreement (SLA):

- **Definition**: A formal agreement that outlines the level of service a customer can expect from a service provider, including performance metrics and responsibilities.

8. Capacity Management:

- **Definition**: The process of ensuring that IT resources are appropriately sized to meet current and future demand, optimizing performance and cost-effectiveness.

9. Availability Management:

- **Definition**: The process of maximizing the availability of IT services by reducing the impact of incidents and problems.

10. IT Service Continuity Management:

- **Definition**: Ensuring that IT services can be restored quickly after a disaster or major disruption.

11. Service Catalog:

- **Definition**: A comprehensive list of IT services available to customers, including descriptions, service levels, and pricing.

12. Change Advisory Board (CAB):

- **Definition**: A group responsible for assessing and approving or rejecting proposed changes to IT services.

13. Knowledge Management:

- **Definition**: The process of capturing, storing, and sharing knowledge and information within an organization to support decision-making and problem-solving.

14. Service Asset and Configuration Management (SACM):

- **Definition**: The process of managing and tracking an organization's assets and configurations, including hardware, software, and documentation.

15. Service Design Package (SDP):

- **Definition**: A document containing all information needed to transition a service into production, including requirements, design, and implementation plans.

16. Service Level Indicator (SLI):

- **Definition**: A metric used to measure the performance of a specific aspect of an IT service, often related to an SLA.

17. Continuous Service Improvement (CSI):

- **Definition**: A core ITIL concept focused on fostering a culture of ongoing improvement in IT services and processes.

18. Service Value System (SVS):

- **Definition**: The overarching model that represents how all the components and activities of ITIL work together to create value for organizations and customers.

19. Service Integration and Management (SIAM):

- **Definition**: An approach to managing multiple service providers and integrating their services to deliver a single, seamless IT service to customers.

20. Agile and DevOps:

- **Definition**: Modern software development and IT

management approaches that emphasize collaboration, speed, and continuous delivery.

This glossary provides a foundation for understanding the language of ITSM and ITIL. As you navigate these frameworks and embark on your journey to IT service excellence, familiarity with these terms will be invaluable in effectively implementing best practices, driving improvement, and aligning IT with your organization's strategic goals.

Resources and References

As you reach the final pages of this book by Nikhilesh Mishra, consider it not an ending but a stepping stone. The pursuit of knowledge is an unending journey, and the world of information is boundless.

Discover a World Beyond These Pages

We extend a warm invitation to explore a realm of boundless learning and discovery through our dedicated online platform: **www.nikhileshmishra.com**. Here, you will unearth a carefully curated trove of resources and references to empower your quest for wisdom.

Unleash the Potential of Your Mind

- **Digital Libraries:** Immerse yourself in vast digital libraries, granting access to books, research papers, and academic treasures.

- **Interactive Courses:** Engage with interactive courses and lectures from world-renowned institutions, nurturing your thirst for knowledge.

- **Enlightening Talks:** Be captivated by enlightening talks delivered by visionaries and experts from diverse fields.

- **Community Connections:** Connect with a global community of like-minded seekers, engage in meaningful discussions, and share your knowledge journey.

Your Journey Has Just Begun

Your journey as a seeker of knowledge need not end here. Our website awaits your exploration, offering a gateway to an infinite universe of insights and references tailored to ignite your intellectual curiosity.

Acknowledgments

As I stand at this pivotal juncture, reflecting upon the completion of this monumental work, I am overwhelmed with profound gratitude for the exceptional individuals who have been instrumental in shaping this remarkable journey.

In Loving Memory

To my father, **Late Shri Krishna Gopal Mishra,** whose legacy of wisdom and strength continues to illuminate my path, even in his physical absence, I offer my deepest respect and heartfelt appreciation.

The Pillars of Support

My mother**, Mrs. Vijay Kanti Mishra,** embodies unwavering resilience and grace. Your steadfast support and unwavering faith in my pursuits have been the bedrock of my journey.

To my beloved wife, **Mrs. Anshika Mishra,** your unshakable belief in my abilities has been an eternal wellspring of motivation. Your constant encouragement has propelled me to reach new heights.

My daughter, **Miss Aarvi Mishra,** infuses my life with boundless joy and unbridled inspiration. Your insatiable curiosity serves as a constant reminder of the limitless power of exploration and discovery.

Brothers in Arms

To my younger brothers, **Mr. Ashutosh Mishra** and **Mr. Devashish Mishra,** who have steadfastly stood by my side, offering unwavering support and shared experiences that underscore the strength of familial bonds.

A Journey Shared

This book is a testament to the countless hours of dedication and effort that have gone into its creation. I am immensely grateful for the privilege of sharing my knowledge and insights with a global audience.

Readers, My Companions

To all the readers who embark on this intellectual journey alongside me, your curiosity and unquenchable thirst for knowledge inspire me to continually push the boundaries of understanding in the realm of cloud computing.

With profound appreciation and sincere gratitude,

Nikhilesh Mishra

September 08, 2023

About the Author

Nikhilesh Mishra is an extraordinary visionary, propelled by an insatiable curiosity and an unyielding passion for innovation. With a relentless commitment to exploring the boundaries of knowledge and technology, Nikhilesh has embarked on an exceptional journey to unravel the intricate complexities of our world.

Hailing from the vibrant and diverse landscape of India, Nikhilesh's pursuit of knowledge has driven him to plunge deep into the world of discovery and understanding from a remarkably young age. His unwavering determination and quest for innovation have not only cemented his position as a thought leader but have also earned him global recognition in the ever-evolving realm of technology and human understanding.

Over the years, Nikhilesh has not only mastered the art of translating complex concepts into accessible insights but has also crafted a unique talent for inspiring others to explore the limitless possibilities of human potential.

Nikhilesh's journey transcends the mere boundaries of expertise; it is a transformative odyssey that challenges conventional wisdom and redefines the essence of exploration. His commitment to pushing the boundaries and reimagining the norm serves as a luminous beacon of inspiration to all those who aspire to make a profound impact in the world of knowledge.

As you navigate the intricate corridors of human understanding and innovation, you will not only gain insight into Nikhilesh's expertise but also experience his unwavering dedication to empowering readers like you. Prepare to be enthralled as he seamlessly melds intricate insights with real-world applications, igniting the flames of curiosity and innovation within each reader.

Nikhilesh Mishra's work extends beyond the realm of authorship; it is a reflection of his steadfast commitment to shaping the future of knowledge and exploration. It is an embodiment of his boundless dedication to disseminating wisdom for the betterment of individuals worldwide.

Prepare to be inspired, enlightened, and empowered as you embark on this transformative journey alongside Nikhilesh Mishra. Your understanding of the world will be forever enriched, and your passion for exploration and innovation will reach new heights under his expert guidance.

Sincerely, **A Fellow Explorer**

Notes

Notes

Notes

Notes

Notes